GIFTS *from the* HEART

Meditations on Caring for Aging Parents

BONNI GOLDBERG
AND GEO KENDALL

CB
CONTEMPORARY BOOKS

Library of Congress Cataloging-in-Publication Data

Goldberg, Bonni.
    Gifts from the heart : meditatations on caring for aging parents /
Bonni Goldberg and Geo Kendall.
        p.   cm.
    Includes index.
    ISBN 0-8092-3143-3
    1. Aging parents—Family relationships.   2. Aging parents—Care.
3. Adult children—Family relationships.   4. Parent and adult child.
5. Caregivers—Psychology.   I. Kendall, Geo.   II. Title.
HQ1063.6.G65   1997
306.874—dc21   97-1491
                                                                      CIP

"Thursday" by Madeleine Mysko. First published in *Hellas* (Fall 1993).
Reprinted by permission of the author.
"Winter Green" by Madeleine Mysko. Reprinted by permission of the author.
"Waltzing in ¾ Time" by Debra Tracey. Reprinted by permission of Debra
Tracey. Copyright © 1996 Mended Dreams Music.

Cover illustration: Copyright © Nicholas Wilton
Cover design by Kim Bartko
Interior design by Mary Lockwood

Copyright © 1997 by Bonni Goldberg and Geo Kendall
Published by Contemporary Books
An imprint of NTC/Contemporary Publishing Company
4255 West Touhy Avenue, Lincolnwood (Chicago), Illinois 60646-1975 U.S.A.
Manufactured in the United States of America
International Standard Book Number: 0-8092-3143-3
15   14   13   12   11   10   9   8   7   6   5   4   3   2   1

To my father,
George W. Kendall, Jr.,
who gave me much more than my name

—GK

To my parents,
Judy and Ivan,
and their parents:
Miriam and Michael Ross and
Florence and Morris Goldberg

—BG

For more information on workshops, lectures, and programs on the gifts of parentcare led by Bonni and Geo, please contact them at:

Full Circle
P. O. Box 50232
Baltimore, MD 21211

Contents

Acknowledgments

Many people contributed to the creation of this book. We would like to thank Kara Leverte, Susan Schwartz, Gerilee Hundt, and Alissa MacMillan, the angel in the office at Contemporary Books; Lisa Swayne, our wonderful agent, and Beth Fighera; Patricia Nitzburg and Julie Convisser for their comments on drafts of the manuscript; Jon Timian for computer help; Debra Tracey, Madeleine Mysko, and Fran Stein for offering their songs, poems, stories, and love; Judy Burch, Don Richardson, Robin Adams Richardson, Beth Lebow, and the staff at Keswick Adult Day Care Center for all their support as Geo cared for his father; David Kendall for being a big brother; the Enoch Pratt Library system—one of the country's best; Chris Maloney and Susan Davis for the rooms to write; our families; and all the wonderful folks who shared their stories with us.

Introductions

Like so many others who care for aging parents, I had to make major adjustments in my life. I had to let go of what was "acceptable." I had to relinquish the view of caregiving as a burden, or as an interruption of the life I'd created. Rather than see caregiving as wrought only with hardships, of which there are plenty, I slowly began to open up to the final gifts that my father was offering me as he declined.

I could have chosen not to be involved, and sometimes I desperately wanted out. But, thankfully, in most of my own darkest moments, often during an insignificant interaction with my father such as combing his hair, I experienced a connection with him, with humanity, and with myself that left me bathed in a glorious warmth.

Each aspect of parentcare called on me to be more responsive to my father's physical and emotional needs as well as my own. Like a child, I had wanted our connection to be on my terms. Through the caregiving experience I discovered that it was I who had to change. I had to have an intimate relationship with someone I had never felt completely comfortable with. I had to reevaluate much of what I took for granted about our bond and how I related to the world I lived in.

This person who created me and with whom I'd had a lifelong link would soon be absent. My father was too busy on this last leg of his life journey to take care of me. I had to follow behind and adapt to seeing him and myself differently. As my father diminished, I gained. In time I realized that we were engaged in the process of an elder passing wisdom on. It was only in retrospect that I understood I'd undergone a similar transaction with my mother years before.

Until my father no longer could care for himself, it was easy for me to mouth an intellectual spirituality that I had adopted over the years, but when it came down to changing my father's underwear, I had to pray in earnest in a new way.

It was from encountering these profound changes in myself that I began to incorporate the experience of parentcare into my work with people, as an artist, and finally to develop the parentcare workshops and groups Bonni and I now conduct.

Aging parents are preparing for their own big journey. As their children we are engaged in the process of taking our new posititon in life at the same time. My hopes in writing this book are that, while accompanying our aging parents to their deaths, we, as the next generation, can open ourselves to receive the wisdom they have accumulated, that we use it well to meet the latter part of our own lives, and that we pass it on to the next in line.

Geo Kendall

As a poet drawn to articulating moments of insight, and as a daughter in preparation for them, I'm compelled to explore the gifts of parentcare: what they are and how to find them.

Because I lent a hand first when Geo cared for his aging father and then when my mother cared for her parents, I was in a unique position to observe how as caregivers they were transformed. As Geo and I canvassed others about their experiences with parentcare, we found that most people also had soul-stirring realizations and personal breakthroughs throughout the process.

In an effort to map an unpredictable journey, we've collected our stories and those of many others, along with our awareness and some of the ways we've achieved it into a series of meditations. Though we have changed names and locales, and sometimes created composites, the narratives are real and true.

Though you may not encounter all the situations within these pages, through the meditations you will become aware that you've embarked on another path, a rite of passage, which will stretch you to your limits and often beyond, but will also feed you in profound ways if you stay alert and open to the gifts you will receive along the way.

It's not our intention to deny or gloss over the difficult and painful aspects of parentcare. Rather we wish to highlight the simultaneous, revelatory gifts that are inherent when you can adjust your perspective to see them. This is the place from which to draw strength and wisdom. Your parents have some final and priceless gifts for you whether they know it or not. As long as *you* know it, those gifts are yours; they will form a bridge. Open your heart. Enter the soul of parentcare. Follow its lead.

Bonni Goldberg

Crossroads

Parentcaring most often enters at your life's mid-point. If it comes earlier, you still may be at a crossroads. Either way, you're in the process of questioning the next phase of your life—the evolution of your career, your opportunity to see more of the world, your financial circumstances, the relationships you've created, the development of your soul. It's neither a coincidence nor an obstacle that when you're evaluating where you've been and where you're going, your association with your parents intensifies.

You're caring for the ones with whom you share genes, legacies, and attitudes, ones who have been the age you are now. Do you remember them at your age? Grappling with some of the same concerns you have currently, they made certain choices. Try not to stand in judgment of your parents' lives. You aren't destined to make similar choices. Your parents' new position in your consciousness, however, will influence the decisions that you make at this juncture. They remain a source of vital information for you.

At this crossroads, I trust that my parents' influence enriches my ability to make choices.

Helping Hands

Because you love your mother doesn't mean you know how to care for her. Caregiving is not something that you innately know how to do; it's an acquired skill. If it takes a whole village—not just a single family—to raise a child, it takes a community or a team to care for elders. Creating partnerships with health care professionals, reliable friends who have some time to give, legal counsel, and state and government agencies is how you build your eldercare community. When you invite others into the intimate parent–child relationship, you invite risk and relief at the same time. The risks include revealing information about your family that until now was private or secret, such as spending or drinking habits. Another risk is that outsiders will be critical of your interactions with your parents and your choices in caring for them. But whatever fears and mistrust emerge in building a team, the relief you'll experience will far outweigh the risks, especially when you include trained professionals and caring friends to advise you and act on your behalf.

With an eldercare team, I get help and the relief that comes with it.

Taking the Torch

If I hear that old story again I'll scream!

How many times have you said this to yourself? Yet storytelling is the oral tradition that records ancestral memories. When the Romans were conquering the nomadic peoples of ancient Europe, one of their tactics was to kill the storyteller of the tribe. This brutal act cut off people from the history of their clan. You may have heard your mother tell the story about her Grandfather Sittig growing a bright orange goatee at age ninety just to torment his wife more times than you care to remember, but can you relate the story with the same vivid detail? Have you considered what the story reveals about your people, or about a quality in yourself? Parents are our link to our family history and traditions, but sooner or later it will be our turn to carry the torch.

Today I take time to make sure I can recount a family story my parent tells; I accept my position as the next storyteller in my family.

New Eyes

Pete's Grille is a neighborhood restaurant that was one of my father's favorite haunts. He would go there a few times a week to have lunch and talk with the other elderly regulars. I'd occasionally stop at Pete's for breakfast. One morning Lou, the owner, asked where my father was. He hadn't been in for a week. Lou said that usually his older customers would let him know if they were going out of town, or into the hospital. Lou and his wife, Char, looked out for the seniors. They offered much more to their elder patrons than the four-dollar senior-citizens' lunch special.

As it turned out, Dad's leg was acting up, and he was resting it by staying home. But he wouldn't have mentioned it to me over the telephone. The incident made me see the neighborhood with new eyes; there was Sharon, the one teller at the bank who took time to go over Dad's statements with him; the mail carrier who knocked on his door if my father hadn't picked up his mail the day before. I noticed the subculture, the subtle network of individuals who took it on themselves to look out for the elderly in small but significant ways. It was the beginning of my conscious role as a provider to my father and to all elders.

My experience of neighborhood community as a source of information and enrichment is broadened as I step into the role of caring for my parents.

Broadsided

"I have my own life!"

"I've got important things to do."

"Why do I have to take care of them? Can't somebody else do it?"

The fact is that most of us are unprepared for this stage of adulthood. We experience it as a shock and as an interruption of our "real" life. Even though we live in an era that values the medical technology that extends life, and there is a general belief that more is better under any circumstance, we don't always anticipate the full consequences of these values.

Because you live in an age in which people live longer, *their* longevity affects the shape of *your* life. Caregiving isn't an intrusion on your destiny. It's a stage of life like college or parenthood, but it doesn't mean you should abandon the existence you've created for yourself. It means another phase with its gifts and burdens is upon you. Caregiving, too, will have a beginning, middle, and an end, and going through it will change you.

I accept this new phase of my life, and I am open to the ways it will change me.

Savoring Memories

Do you remember idolizing your parents? There was a time when in your eyes they could do no wrong.

I remember watching my mother hanging up clothes on the line and thinking she was the most beautiful woman in the world. To this day, when I smell clean clothes from an outdoor line I experience a moment of bliss.

These moments can't be diminished by time or circumstance. They still have a visceral effect on you. They only become painful when you long to repeat them, yet understand their return is not possible. By savoring these incidents you can draw on the sense of well-being they engender. They're a resource for the renewal of the bond between you and your parents—for each of you. Positive memories, if you use them this way, will carry you through many difficult times as you practice parentcare in the present.

Today I savor a memory for the sense of well-being that it engenders in me.

Where and When They Enter

My mother is a fit and active woman in her sixties. There's very little she can't or won't do. She lives on her own in a big city and enjoys a full professional and social life. During the past year her home was robbed while she was out, and she dislocated her shoulder while trying to prevent a man from snatching her purse. It isn't that my mother is frail or unalert. The city in which she lives is fiercer, more predatory than it was when she was in her middle years. She isn't accustomed to taking the precautions my women friends take these days. It's hard for her to shift her style of living, even in the wake of the year's incidents. I'm not sure she would consider being increasingly cautious and afraid an acceptable form of living. She feels territorial: this is my city, my home, nobody pushes me around or out of it. I've been here my whole life—I'm a tough cookie. She doesn't see that she's prone to being victimized because she doesn't feel like an old woman.

I can't expect her to change overnight if, indeed, she changes at all. I discuss my concerns with her and strategies that might make her less vulnerable. But, finally, I must let her make her own way as she has had to let me make mine.

Today I do what I can to protect my parents and then I let go.

The Mind's Eye

There is an image of each of your parents that you hold in your mind. It's usually what they looked like during your childhood or early adolescence. As both you and your parents age, you make minor adjustments to that picture: a little less hair, a few more wrinkles, looser skin. But there comes a point when your parents' physical appearance is dramatically different. Traces of your mental picture remain but it's as if your real-life mother and father are being covered up or exaggerated.

It can take time to become comfortable touching or kissing these otherworldly versions of your parents. They may not recognize themselves, either. At first, you may view the changes as chilling and repulsive. They're also opportunities to release both you and your parents from your judgments about how all of you should appear in life.

Each time I gaze at my parents' physical transformations, I make room for change.

Silent Treatment

I remember all the times that people turned their eyes from my father when he asked for anything beyond their comfort level. He would get so frustrated when he was being ignored. He was old but he knew what was going on. Sometimes it took him a whole day to ride the bus downtown, stand in line at an agency or bank, and reach the desk only to be told that he lacked a necessary form or that the clerk was out of the forms and he would have to come back tomorrow. Because I was his advocate, I had to step in on many occasions to make sure that he was heard. But I had to do it in a way that was respectful of him and that didn't insult his intelligence. Everyone had an excuse for why they had failed to take the time to listen to him and help him out, but most of the time it was because he was old. I knew that I, too, had done my share of ignoring old people.

Through caring for my father, I tuned into the often quirky communication styles of elders and the uncanny fullness I experienced in my heart when I took the extra moments to hear them out and do what I could to help them.

I take the time to tune into all the elders I encounter today.

"They're Just Like Children"

The concept that caring for an elderly parent is like caring for a child is a fallacy. It arises out of the assumption that only one type of dependency exists and so only one method of caregiving is available. We also have a tendency to refer back to familiar experiences when we are faced with frightening new ones. Sometimes this impulse limits our perspective.

Children's dependency is entirely different from that of elderly adults. Children are growing, developing, and learning. Elders are approaching death. It's a joyful moment when you see a child awaken to a new stage of development. A child's first steps and first words have an impact different from a parent's first missed step or first lost word.

When you accept parentcare as its own unique form of interdependency, then each phase of the process becomes an exchange between you and your parent. You're caregiving, and in return your parent is engaging you in new nuances of interconnection.

In the realm of parentcare, I am also an explorer discovering insights that I will draw from during my own living and dying.

Flowers and Weeds

Given the challenges of caring for a parent, to some the task may seem to be an unfair and unnecessary hardship. Like a vacant lot, parentcare is at first glance unsightly and full of weeds. But as you continue to observe the lot, pastel blue flowers stand out. These are the blooms of the chicory plant, whose roots were used by Native Americans to make a drink similar to coffee. Weed or soothing drink, the worth of the blue chicory flower is relative to how you understand it. It's this way with parentcare. The value often isn't apparent to you in the middle of certain situations, but you eventually get to the essence of the experience.

I hang tough today until I understand something new about my parent or myself.

"Respect Your Elders"

You've heard this phrase your whole life, but what does it really mean? We don't always agree on what qualities merit respect. And we talk about respect as something that each of us deserves while we realize that it must be earned.

What do you respect about your parents? Are these lasting qualities or ones that wane with age and loss of abilities? Perhaps you are discovering new things to respect about them: tenacity, tenderness, wisdom. How is this new stage of your relationship with your parents challenging your notions of respect?

I affirm the new ways I'm learning to respect my parents and myself.

Family Ties

Carmen had a stormy relationship with her parents. She decided to look elsewhere among her relatives for a sense of family. She traveled a long distance to visit a great-aunt whom she'd never met before. Aunt Florence was eighty-nine years old and had lost much of her mobility. Florence made small talk for three hours. Carmen struggled with boredom but did her best to stay attentive. As Carmen prepared to leave, her Aunt Florence looked her in the eyes and said, "Why do you love me?" Carmen was speechless. Did she love this woman she barely knew? Then, as the tears welled up, she answered: "Because you're my great-aunt!" Carmen's pilgrimage brought her to understand the power of blood ties. It had not only caused her to make the journey, but it had stirred up a level of love in her that was neither rational nor within her control.

I acknowledge the call of blood ties as beyond my control.

Elder-in-Waiting

Caring for your parents will lead you to consider the kind of elder person you will become. You have recognized many of your personality traits, and you've noticed how age accentuates them: your parents are your examples. They also show you the benefits of being older. For instance, they may speak their minds regardless of propriety. As an elder-in-waiting, this is something you can look forward to.

My parents are still helping me learn how to be in the world. Today I consider the benefits of being an elder myself.

How Do I Do It?

While it's true that the elderly population is increasing, it's also true that aged parents have always been in our midst. How did people cope? Look around at your own family: grandparents, great-aunts and great-uncles. How did your parents and their siblings and spouses handle eldercare? Whatever your family legacy is in this area, it's your turn to add to it.

The poet Rumi says, "Let the beauty we love be what we do." Your contribution to eldercare will be most meaningful if you base it on your circumstances and your personal values. An honest evaluation of the pros and cons of the ways your people coped before you is energy better spent than worrying over what your family will think of your choices. You must answer the call of parentcare by being truly authentic. It's possible that caregiving is calling to you to contemplate your personal development.

I make caregiving an extension of who I am, or who I am in the process of becoming.

Generations

Children's views about old people come from their personal relationships to them. As a child I accompanied my mother once a week to visit Great-Aunt Glade in a nursing home. Although most of the time Glade was noncommunicative, there was another woman at the home with long braids of gray hair and sparkling blue eyes. She had been a teacher. Every week she held my hand and asked me all about school. As the middle child in a family of five, I rarely got the individual attention she showed me. My experience with her made me comfortable relating to old people for the rest of my life. My mother gave me a great gift by exposing me to relationships with elders. In return she received the gift of my comfort with old people during her later years.

I remember an elder I related to as a child and carry the sense of ease and admiration with me as I interact with my parents.

Finding What You Didn't Lose

There was no way around it. While caring for my parents, the ways I was like them became glaringly obvious to me: both the negatives and the positives. Our similarity is one of the reasons my parents turned out to be among my greatest teachers. Although I'd always been known as one who easily expresses his feelings, I realized through being in close contact with my father again that, like the salesman he was, I could talk convincingly but was emotionally distant. As my father became increasingly ill, some of his barriers to emotional exchanges came down. I saw myself twenty-five years from now, wishing I had loved more freely. This realization propelled me to start knocking down my own barriers.

Today my parent has something to show me about myself. I'm ready to see it.

Losing It

A nger, rage:
   "Don't treat me like a child!"
"Don't touch me. I hate you!"
"I'll kill you! I'll call the police!"

Especially in the context of dementia, deep-seated anger often erupts into intense battles of will. You may lose it and become just as angry and out of control as your parent. She might focus and obsess on her anger, accelerating it into a rage.

You are not the reason for your parent's anger. She is not the reason for yours. You are both angry about the situation. You can't always quell this deep and powerful emotion.

Our powerful anger is an affirmation of the strength of both our spirit and our desire for life.

Psychobabble

Analyzing your parents is just another way of keeping an emotional distance from them. You think that understanding their psychology will give you a sense of control over your reactions to them. Your relationship with them is so much more than the combination of your subconscious mechanisms. The mind can be a thief, a quick-change crook concocting a psychological profile with one hand while stealing the intelligence of experience with the other.

🎁 *Today I seek understanding beyond the limits of my own thinking.*

Missing Links

Why should you go to all the trouble of bringing your elder parents to every celebration? In some cultures there is no celebration without the presence of the elders. There's a reason for this. When you take your father to his great-grand-niece's naming ceremony and he holds the baby, a circle has been completed. When you bring your mother to her granddaughter's graduation party, she glides into the memories of all the adolescent relatives, perhaps to surface later as a source of strength and wonder. Your parents are links.

Although I was a child and only met her a few times, my Great-Grand-Aunt Rose left an impression on me. When my Great-Aunt Esther is present at an important event, as the oldest member of our family, she engenders an alchemy.

When you bring your elder to a celebration, you offer so much more than the present you've brought or the check you've written.

I turn away from my ego's desire not to be bothered toward my soul's need for connection.

In the Absence of Love

There's a big difference between being very angry with your parents and not loving them. Still, certain conditions and behaviors can result in an absence of love between a child and a parent. You don't have to love your parents to be a caregiver. You can arrange their care rather than doing it yourself.

You also can offer hands-on care for your own sake. If you choose this path, you will be doing it to complete your role as the archetypal Daughter or Son to an archetypal Mother or Father. Under these circumstances your actions aren't in response to your particular parents. You're also not acting out of a sense of duty to them but rather out of a duty to yourself to complete a certain cycle of life. You act because you believe it's necessary and valuable to prepare for what's ahead. You've made a valid choice, and it can be fruitful. Your commitment may be harder to sustain over time, but it isn't impossible.

There's also the decision not to offer any type of care whatsoever. If you make this choice, explore offering caregiving to another elder family member, or volunteer at a nursing home or elder day care center, so you don't deprive yourself of participating in this crucial juncture of your life cycle.

Caring for elders is one of my rites of passage.

Sacrifice

Is parentcare a sacrifice? Absolutely. But is it a deprivation? The word *sacrifice* is derived from the word *sacred*. It means to make sacred. So it's a kind of offering. The dictionary defines *sacrifice* as the giving up of a thing for the sake of another. What if that "other" was your most authentic self? Whenever you give up something in your life, you make room for another thing. So sacrifice is as much a gain as a loss, as well as a process of making something sacred.

Through parentcare you're sacrificing your limited ways of being. You're shedding attitudes, beliefs, and rigidity. Many people mistakenly sacrifice their friendships, careers, and creativity in the name of parentcare. These things are easier to give up, less challenging to your ego that wants you to believe you are, at your essence, your thoughts, feelings, and actions.

The main thing we fear from our sacrifices is losing our self. This fear is a form of scarcity thinking—scarcity of self. You don't have to sacrifice your "inner child" or your integrity, but you may make them sacred by sacrificing the way you perceive them.

Today, through parentcare, I sacrifice one belief that no longer serves me.

Maneuvers

When I lived 3,000 miles from my parents and came to visit, it was always a shock to me how aging had affected both of them. On my final trip, I arrived just in time to help my father take my mother to an emergency doctor's appointment. Dad was very agitated and entirely focused on keeping track of my mother's purse and figuring out the fastest route to the doctor's office. The three of us were standing in a line on the porch—my mother, my father, and me—when my mother turned a pasty shade of white and collapsed. To catch her, I had to maneuver around my father who was so engrossed in the directions he had scrawled on a grocery receipt that he hadn't noticed she'd fainted.

In the weeks that followed, my mother declined, and my father, blind to his own limits, resisted my help. Having been her life partner and sole caregiver, he often tried to prevent me from having access to my mother, claiming she was asleep or too weak for me to visit. Throughout her illness, I would return to that moment on the porch. As on that day, I often had to maneuver around my father to reach her.

🎁 *My ability to maneuver is one of my caregiving tools.*

Family Dynamics

As one of the primary caregivers, you may find yourself in the position of having to delegate certain tasks to other family members, expecting that they will carry out your instructions smoothly and efficiently. This expectation may not be realistic.

Even in the closest family, caregiving presents hidden difficulties. Most of our families aren't model families and few of us have been taught cooperative caregiving skills.

Each family member has a unique dynamic with your parent. Unfinished business, immaturities, addictions, the fear of one's own death, and illness shape how individual family members deal with the situation and each other. All the family dynamics surface and, like a mobile with a newly missing piece, spin wildly until a new balance is established.

I only have to live up to the expectations I place on myself.

Bare Essentials

Eek! A naked parent! I had to elicit the aid of a neighbor when it was time to bathe my mother. The first time I helped my father into the shower I looked away; he was the type who wouldn't even walk around the house in his underwear. Our culture has taught us that an aging body is something to fight and avoid. It's a bit unnerving to see your parents naked—flabby, vulnerable, discolored—much less interact with them in their state of nakedness.

More is revealed to you than body parts. There lies the future of your body; don't give in to fear. Look as mortality smiles at you.

I witness my parents' metamorphosis in preparation for my own.

Eye to Eye

We gaze into the eyes of our beloved to be closer and feel more deeply connected. We speak with our eyes to our children, friends, even strangers in a language more poignant than words. When was the last time you really looked into your parent's eyes and allowed her to look into yours without averting your gaze? It isn't necessarily easy, and you might feel uncomfortable at first, but an unspoken message is awaiting you each time you look deeply.

I was forty-five years old before I realized my father's eyes were a mix of green and soft gray. When my heart was open, I could see the tears welling in his eyes. It's said that the eyes are the windows to our soul.

Today I gaze into my elder's eyes for more than just a moment.

Value

Time isn't really money. It's time. But it is extremely valuable; you only have a certain amount of it. If you look at the hours spent caring for your parents as time or money lost, you will find yourself resentful.

Your belief that your time is spent better doing one thing over another—going sailing over folding your parents' laundry—confuses the particulars of what you do with the true purpose of your time. For instance, if you believe your time is for the purpose of pleasure then don't waste your time seeking it, instead find pleasure in what you're doing right now.

🎁 *Today, while caregiving, I will look for where the true value lies for me.*

Dancing Lessons

In "Waltzing in ¾ Time," singer-songwriter Debra Tracey uses learning to dance as a metaphor for life after losing a loved one. In many ways the song also captures the "dance" of an aging parent and a loving daughter looking out for him, especially if you think of the wife in the song as a symbol for lost youth or abilities:

> *He was her partner, she was his wife:*
> *A memory that I can still see.*
> *But the dance that they danced most of their lives*
> *Wasn't always meant to be.*
> *When she passed away he had to stay,*
> *Finding himself all alone.*
> *But no shy man is he, no stranger to friends,*
> *He soon found himself a new home:*
> *Where he learned about fox-trots, merengues and*
> *   box steps,*
> *Found people to dance with galore,*
> *Started feeling new rhythms, and learning new patterns,*
> *   And moving around on the floor.*

Chorus:

And he's waltzing in ¾ time.
And her memory still dances in and out of his mind.
And he's waltzing, he's waltzing,
He's waltzing in ¾ time.

So different at first, the feel of all this:
So many new things to learn.
Step this way on the third beat, and don't watch your
* feet;*
Look out, there's that one tricky turn.
He learned the new dance, how to dance by himself,
Perhaps a new partner he'll find.
Sometimes it's awkward, sometimes he stumbles;
Right now he's doing just fine.
So for today, I celebrate with him.
And I smile as I watch him waltzing in ¾ time.

🎁 *Today I appreciate the ways my parents and I are*
adjusting to this new dance.

Limitations

The first signs that my father was not quite his old self appeared at least three years before he was officially diagnosed with dementia. I was working on a renovation job and often brought my father along to help; he was retired, loved to work with his hands, and liked the cash. The job site was in a neighborhood he knew well. At lunchtime he went to pick up our sandwiches at the deli a few blocks away. Two hours later, he returned frazzled and upset; he had gotten lost.

The people we were working for, a registered nurse and a psychiatrist, mentioned tactfully that it appeared that my father was having a real problem. I defended him, saying he was having a bad day because it was near the anniversary of my mother's death. My gut told me, however, that beneath my excuse for his actions lay the gnawing truth.

There is no shame in not acting on the early signs of your parent's new limits. *If only* and *I should have* thoughts serve no useful purpose. They only sap your much-needed energy. There is no "right" way to break through denial.

I accept my way of moving through denial. My pace is a strength in certain areas of my life.

Parent Partnerships

You're entering a new phase of relationship with your parents. No longer the child, the rebellious teen, the young adult forging your own life, you've reentered the relationship as helpmate and advocate. Even in a dysfunctional family where you might have been a junior dad or mom, your role is different now. All of you will need to adjust to being in partnership.

At no other time in life do most parents and children interact as partners. It feels odd introducing this new dimension into your relationship. You may need to enlist the help of another—a relative, a social worker, or clergy—to intercede.

Think about your most successful collaborative efforts that worked in *process* as well as for an end result. One person cannot be in a position of authority over the other. Working partnerships can include setting goals *together* and being clear about who does what, but your parents may have a different style of working in partnership than you do, or they may only feel secure accomplishing things independently. You can't be in a genuine partnership with them unless you can meet them at a point of compromise. And you may be the one who has to make the most concessions.

I interact with my parents today, mindful that we're all adjusting to being in partnership.

More Limits

It's not your job to convince your parents of their lessening abilities. Even after the doctor told my father directly that he had signs of dementia, my father chose to hear only that he was *physically* fit. He was adamant in his belief that the doctors didn't really know what they were talking about, that he knew himself best, and that he was fine. He was so persuasive in his self-assured, parental tone of voice that sometimes *I* believed him, until another event occurred that demonstrated otherwise. Then I redoubled my efforts to get him to face his situation because I didn't want to go through the painful cycle of hope and disappointment one more time. Finally, I had to face *my own* limitations in bringing my father around to seeing his situation my way.

I accept my own limitations as well as those of my parent's.

Hoary People

In our sanitized vision of the world, people grow old and die in their sleep looking much like they did their whole lives. But some people reach a stage of hoariness that all your tending can't mask or prevent. They are transforming into the earth.

Hoary means impressively or venerably old, ancient. Your parents actually emanate great beauty and wisdom in this state. Their wrinkles are mountain crags, the tufts of hair grown on the edges of their ears are brush, their gnarly veins are tangled vines or roots.

At the same time you are being called to refocus your vision. Like an artist might, begin to see these once familiar faces as landscapes. Then after your parents die, you will be able to find them in parks or meet them in forests whenever you need to.

🎁 *Today I see the world where hoary people have an important place.*

Living Legends

Who can put a price on the value of one person's life experience? Your parents are living documents of the history that they've lived through. One of the gifts of spending concentrated time with your parents when you're an adult is that you begin to assemble a broader sense of them. Your child's slanted perspective is widened. Whether it was prop planes, moon walks, home canning, frozen dinners, satellite dishes, or heart transplants, your parents witnessed phases of history firsthand. They can provide you with a perspective unmatched by history books or scholars. They're living treasures: your personal link to a period of time with significant ramifications in your own life today.

When taking time to talk with my parents about their era, I receive a priceless perspective on today.

The Eldercare Machine

Sometimes I feel as though there's an eldercare machine that uses old people for fuel, chews them up, and spits them out. It turns out that my parents have the wrong kind of health insurance and the wrong kind of wills, and they received the wrong advice. My parents have had to work the machine using the wrong operating instructions. Now I'm the one who's their advocate, but the rules and regulations keep changing. I have to keep pace with my parents' needs and the great machine.

Yesterday when I was in the geriatric wing of the hospital, I overheard a nurse explaining to an irate couple that the staff had "temporarily misplaced" their father. I wanted to scream. So I did. I got into my car, drove to the far end of a shopping mall lot, and with all the windows rolled up I let out several bloodcurdling yells. After I caught my breath, I went into the mall and sat down for a cup of herbal tea and a cookie. I knew I couldn't slay the machine, but I wasn't going to let it slay me, either.

I may lose a battle now and then, but I win the war against total despair.

Opening the Gate

A friend of ours who works in an eldercare center observed that families who attend the center's support groups for caregivers handle better the ever-shifting condition of their elders than families that don't. Letting other families in on what you view as the weaknesses of your family may seem at first to be against the instinct of protecting blood, tribe, or community at all costs. But there are gifts to be received when you allow the wisdom of others' experience in. Witnessing another clan move through a hard situation is more meaningful than anything you can read about coping with it. And sharing your experience is a way to return the favor by helping other families.

🎁 *My family is part of a larger family.*

Clues *me!*

Once you're involved in your parent's care, the process of information gathering begins. It's a maze with many twists and turns and sometimes it may seem that the Minotaur is around the next bend. Whether you need information about retirement communities, hospice care, or health insurance, it isn't always forthcoming. At times it seems like a Sisyphean task to get information from a bureaucratic agency.

I learned the vinegar-or-honey method. After failed attempts at gathering information by demanding, complaining, and huffing (vinegar), I began to cultivate patience and courtesy (honey) toward the person on the other end of the telephone who put me on hold, forgot about me, or transferred me to the wrong extension. Eventually, I would prevail.

Throughout our lives we gather information to move us forward. Collecting data is a creative act. Information gathering satisfies an aspect of our curious nature, which has greatly influenced the survival of our species. There's a spirit to the gathering of information. It allows us to partake in the thrill of success when the information congeals into what we want to know rather than getting stuck in the frustration of getting there.

🎁 *While information gathering, I focus on my natural curiosity.*

A Place in Time: Yielding

St. Petersburg, Florida, is referred to as the town of the newly wed and the nearly dead. I moved there from the young city of Austin, Texas. The elder population was double that of the newlyweds. No matter what the situation—at a store, driving, having a conversation—I found myself waiting for an elderly person.

At first, I was full of impatience and anxiety. But because there was nothing I could do about the pace, I started to experiment with what I could do with the time. I took deep breaths and really looked around me. I started to feel intensely present. I noticed more of the details of my surroundings. I became more aware of what I was feeling and thinking. I struck up conversations with the others in line and learned about some hidden spots to visit. Without the assistance of a guru, therapist, or philosopher, the elder residents of St. Pete taught me a lesson.

When it came time to care for my father, I'd already learned how to take a moment for myself while waiting for him. I couldn't always do it, but when I did I felt a peace my busy life couldn't provide me. In this way, caring for my father became caring for myself.

Being busy isn't always a bad thing, but through my elders I find the space to move to a different rhythm for a while.

Disappearing Act

You may notice that some people who were a part of your parents' lives are becoming less available or are just plain disappearing. These are the folks who have difficulty facing aging. You probably feel angry at their desertion, even if you understand their motives. You also may feel envious of their ability to turn away.

Understanding something doesn't necessarily shift your feelings nor should it always have that effect. Emotions are one of your tools for evaluating your situation. Remember that caregiving is a matter of choice. You, too, could choose to step back or disappear at any time.

Today I revisit the reasons why I choose to stay involved in caregiving. If necessary, I readjust the degree or method of my involvement.

Visual Aids

During the period of time you care for your parents, they have a new status in your life. Reminders of your current role in their lives, and theirs in yours, will help you to grasp and hold on to your new position. Visual aids help. Locate a place in your home—it doesn't have to be very large. Use it as a source of reinforcing your new relationship with them. In this space place whatever photographs, plants, sayings, and objects that support the aspects of your current connection to each other that you most value. Take a few minutes, daily if you can, to look over these reminders or to meditate near them. Some people put theirs on the dashboard of their car so that on their way back and forth from visiting their parents they can affirm their intentions at every red light.

I can use visual aids to remind me of my intentions in caring for my parents.

On the Job

Craig and Nancy own a store where they sell antique prints and do framing. While I was in the store one day, an old gentleman in an outdated suit approached me and said he was Craig's father. He explained that he often helped his son with the accounting. John was eighty-nine years old. Later in the week I stopped in, and John was wrapping prints in clear plastic. He looked thoroughly engrossed in his work.

Whether John is an accountant or a print wrapper, Craig and Nancy appreciate his need to be useful and productive. Part of caring for him includes letting him help them. John may be slower and more difficult in some ways than a younger employee or someone outside of the family, but he's also willing and dependable. Craig and Nancy understand that feeling valuable is as essential to well-being as food.

Whether through a task, a question, or some advice, I sincerely let my parents help me today.

Forgiveness

It takes effort to forgive someone. It doesn't just happen over time like curing firewood. But it usually takes the greater effort not to forgive. As it sinks in that your elder parents have limited time left, old hurts may resurface along with your desire to absolve them.

In our experience it's only possible to begin the process when you no longer feel diminished by the person who you feel has wronged you, or if you develop the perspective that the person was only the messenger and not the message.

Parents are the hardest people to forgive and not to forgive. Ultimately, your greatest motivation to pardon them is a selfish one: to free yourself from the pain. Sometimes it's possible to exonerate the person without excusing the deed.

Today I make an effort to forgive my parents to free myself.

Becoming an Authority

It is beneficial to become knowledgeable about aging and caregiving. Many helpful books are available. But sometimes in your attempt to be the best caregiver, you plunge into the information and become an instant authority. Knowledge is a double-edged sword.

It is important to know what you are up against, but you may find yourself overflowing with a litany of symptoms, diagnoses, and stages that you recite to anyone who asks you how it's going. Your recitation can overwhelm others and depress you. Sometimes details and information mask your need for support from friends and family.

I admit to being overwhelmed. I can shift from relating the details of my parent's condition to my friends to sharing my feelings.

Worry

Lately, every time Jean visits her folks they ask her to do some errands for them because the store, three blocks away, is too far for them to walk. For the first time in her life Jean worries about her parents.

As we commiserated, the conversation turned back to worry. Neither of us was accustomed to that state of mind. We agreed it was uncomfortable, at times downright painful, and always exhausting. What was underneath the worry? Jean said love, and I added concern.

Our experience of love was the opposite of worry. It filled us up and gave us energy. So we both decided to experiment. When we fell into worry about our folks, we would try to consciously flip it over into a focused meditation on our feelings of love for them: we would try to visualize the love—smell it, taste it, hear it, and feel it as an entity, a force. When we compared results, we both found that when we made the effort to concentrate, the worry dissipated and we felt more deeply connected to our parents and to our own lives.

Today I will worry less and love more.

The Old and the New

The exchange between children and elders is crucial to both. The people of Burkina Faso, in Africa, believe that when elders die they release their spirits into the young. In all cultures, a unique energy is passed between elder and child. Whether the relationship is affectionate or standoffish, old and young are enlightened by one another. In the presence of the child, the elder stays connected and in touch with the present and the future. In the company of the elder, the child sees past his parents' limits and expectations.

Just as beginnings and endings share similarities, those just entering life and those preparing to leave it meet in the place where boundaries and expectations dissolve and they wink at each other.

By bringing them together, I provide my elders and my children with something I can't give either.

Who Said?

We've become adults during a period of history in which our society places the highest value on individual achievement, ambition, material gain, and what is termed freedom—meaning the ability to do as we please when we please. While there are gains we've made with these standards, there are many setbacks.

In some part because of these values, at each juncture in your life you have an opportunity to reevaluate the principles you live by and decide which to abandon, which new ones to embrace, and which ones to revise.

The period of parentcare is no exception. You shed your current skin in favor of a new one. Many of the outward changes will be out of necessity, but internal shifts—developing a true appreciation for how parentcare is transforming you—is something that takes a desire and an effort on your part.

Today I consider the new values that parentcare presents to me.

Respecting Solitude

It is easy to overlook a parent's need for solitude. At first, I thought my parents would be glad to see me whenever I stopped by. I'd temporarily fallen back into a child/parent relationship with them. The first time my father closeted himself in the bedroom when I arrived for a visit my feelings were hurt. But I got it. They needed their time alone without interruption. Mom's afternoons in the garden snipping her overmanicured hedges were important to her.

Elder parents have a lot to contemplate. They may not always enjoy the nature of what they muse about, but muse they must. Respecting their private time is a sign that you value their individuality.

Your parents may not be able to tell you that you're interrupting their seclusion or they may be acclimated to foregoing their wants for those of their children. You might want to let them know that you're aware of their needs, and that you wish to be sensitive to them.

Recognizing my parents' need for solitude reminds me of my own need for the same.

Beneath the Anger

All by itself, anger is a legitimate feeling to experience and to express. It's important to release it or it turns on you to make you physically ill and spills over onto unsuspecting and undeserving people who just happen to be in the wrong place at the wrong time. Then you feel guilty, too.

The brand of anger I experienced while I was involved in parentcare was multilayered. Often I was mad about the situation rather than with a particular person or event. I released my pent-up rage about how unfair the situation was through speed-walking or by throwing bigger and bigger rocks into a stream—one for each thing with which I was angry. I found myself experiencing waves of fear, guilt, helplessness, and hurt, along with my ire. Beneath my anger lay a river of emotions I could often release only by attending to the wrath that served as its messenger.

I delve beneath anger today.

A Wing and a Prayer

There are many definitions of prayer: petition, praise, thanks, supplication, a spiritual communion, a craving, a negligible hope or chance. Caring for your parents presents many opportunities for the gambit of prayers. Whether you are religious or not, you will find prayer a vital tool for caregiving.

One way to think of prayer is as a way to get outside of the limited self that only has so much time, patience, and courage. You're connecting to the collective flow of life. It's an immediate way to draw on the additional energy you need or to see the bigger picture so you can proceed. You don't have to put your hands together, get on your knees, address a deity, or be respectful or serious in tone to pray. You just have to want some extra help.

Today I take the time to pray as much as I need to and in whatever way feels true to me.

Boredom

Blair is a vibrant and active woman in her mid-sixties who has arthritis in her knees. She has been advised not to hike or go for long walks, which are her favorite activities. Blair has become bored and frustrated. Her husband and children encourage her to fight the arthritis with physical therapy and diet, but it isn't in her nature to stand up to a prognosis. The family has tried to introduce Blair to different activities, but she isn't motivated to develop new interests.

After several unsuccessful attempts, the family has given up trying to engage her. Although they're available for her, they've left Blair to find her own way through her anger and despair to reconnect to her enjoyment of life.

It's hard on her family to step back and endure Blair's complaints and her envy toward them for having greater mobility. It's hard on them also to think that she might not recover from her boredom. But just as the family can't convince her to face her arthritis their way, they have to honor her method and pace of coping, and work through their own feelings about her arthritis.

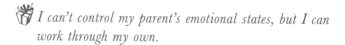 *I can't control my parent's emotional states, but I can work through my own.*

Sexual Healing

You probably have noticed that your sexual energy is much different than it was in the past. Sexual energy ebbs and flows throughout your life and it is no different for our elders. In fact, often elders with dementia have heightened sexual desires and less inhibitions about expressing them. While it often is difficult to imagine your parents having sex, they do, and now they may be quite candid about their feelings and exploits. You may feel embarrassed by your parents' talk or actions, even a little competitive if they seem to have more interest in sex at their age than you do at yours. Remember that desire is an aspect of the life force that surges through all living beings. Think of your parents' increased libido as a way the body compensates for losing other abilities or means of giving and receiving pleasure.

Sexual desire is proof of the life force that still courses through my parents who deserve pleasure, nurturing, and intimacy.

Scam Busters

It's not always possible to protect your parents from the onslaught of wheeler-dealers: high-pressure telephone solicitations, direct-mail advertising that resembles bills, door-to-door hustlers. Certain people have no qualms about taking advantage of others. It makes sense to be angry and frustrated when you discover your parents lost money in a scam. But with whom are you angry? Your first impulse may be to blame your parents: berate them, speak to them in a disdainful or patronizing tone, pronounce unreasonable rules such as no talking on the telephone to strangers. Your image of them as capable and sound has been affronted once again. Or maybe you blame yourself because you couldn't protect your parents despite your careful planning and hard work. It's disheartening. Your fears resurface.

Once your parents did their best to protect you, and despite their efforts they didn't always succeed. In the face of their limits, perhaps they felt the same way that you do now.

Take action. Direct the anger to where it belongs: at the scam artist. Report the incident to the authorities. Remember that even the most cautious and alert people get duped now and then.

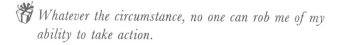 *Whatever the circumstance, no one can rob me of my ability to take action.*

The Odyssey

After Stanley's mother, Sandra, was diagnosed with dementia, she insisted on making a trip to Eastern Europe where both her parents were born. Stanley felt the physical and emotional toll would be great on both of them. Finally, Sandra persuaded him to accompany her on the trip.

It was a difficult journey. Sandra tired easily, was often irritable, and already was showing signs of memory loss. At the same time, they located the hamlet where her mother had lived, they walked among the gravestones of great-great-grandparents, and they dined with a distant cousin.

The trip had a profound impact on Stanley and his sense of place in the world. Sandra had shaken her fist at dementia and had taken a stand of independence before accepting the loss of her faculties, and she had stepped further back in time than even her fully functioning memory could have taken her. In these ways, it was a homecoming of the soul for both son and mother.

In the months that followed, Sandra's memory continued to weaken. Although she often confused the timing of her trip, she referred to it until her death, and every time she mentioned it Stanley felt a rush of gratitude that he'd agreed to make the journey.

 Today I follow the lead of the soul—my parent's or my own.

The Darkest Shadow

I was on the roof patching a spot and clearing the gutters of leaves. Dad insisted on helping. He recently had been diagnosed as having dementia, and it had just dawned on me that I was his primary caregiver.

I was using a heavy crowbar to pull some nails. Dad was bent over clearing a gutter. His back was toward me. I thought for an instant that with one blow I could knock him off the roof. It would look like an accident. He wouldn't have to suffer from losing his mind and I wouldn't have to suffer taking care of him.

The crowbar burned in my hands. My temples throbbed. I couldn't believe it; I wanted to kill him.

My thoughts frightened me. I flung the bar over the edge of the roof and sat down. My father was working away, oblivious to my murderous plot. "Hey Dad," I called out, "let's have some lunch."

"OK," he said, "if *you're* hungry we'll take a break."

Later, I admitted my experience to a friend. I was sure she would think me a monster. Instead she confided that she had a similar moment when she had to leave the room to control her urge to suffocate her sleeping father with a pillow. Primitive passions and our darkest shadows often are awakened by caregiving.

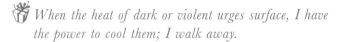 *When the heat of dark or violent urges surface, I have the power to cool them; I walk away.*

Women's Work Is Never Done

Statistically, the role of caregiver falls on the eldest daughter, or if the eldest child is a son, it falls on his wife. Plenty of sons participate in eldercare, but for the most part the primary caregiver is a woman.

Women have been taught to nurture more than men. This fact doesn't mean that women prefer to nurture above all else. It does mean that expectations—theirs and men's—run along the lines that a woman is better at care. There's also an assumption made by both sexes that women are better able to manage care along with some combination of a career, mothering, civic activities, a romantic relationship, and caring for herself.

While an ability to nurture others can enrich one's life, this truth isn't confined to women. In many cases, the most practical solution turns out to be for the woman to take on the primary care, but it's never beneficial for her to take it on exclusively.

When women liberate themselves from the assumption that they will be the only caregiver, they liberate other members of their family from a closed system of thinking and problem solving.

Everyone, regardless of gender, age, or circumstance, benefits from participating in eldercare.

Give and Take

As you witness your parents aging and dying, you brush up against your own mortality. Will your experience be like theirs? There's no way to predict how you'll feel as you age, but your participation in parent-care will influence your own elder years. Each situation you face with your parents, each observation you make as they cope with their feelings, adds to your understanding. Through caring for them you're preparing for your own turn.

Although I live one day at a time, each day prepares me for tomorrow.

Natural Resources

To regenerate and invigorate the caregiving spirit, there is no place better to go than a favorite spot in nature. You don't have to arrange a week away at the beach or the mountains. An afternoon hike or an hour in the garden will suffice. Nature not only offers incredible grandeur but also the small silent spaces where reflection and wisdom abound.

Nowhere are life cycles so clear as in trees: seedling, sapling, young tree, mature tree, ancient tree, decaying tree blending into the earth and nurturing the next generation. Old trees carry their life stories in the twists and turns they have made in seeking the sun. They carry the scars of storms and disease. They house many other lives: moss, vines, insects, reptiles, and mammals. Similar to a tree, you stand in the midst of your life, rooted to your family.

It's reassuring to find wisdom and peace through something as basic as a large boulder or a slab of stone baking in the sun as you sense its cool center, or by lying beside a gurgling creek, watching the butterflies drink on the muddy banks. Even a walk through a winter wood crystallizes your sense of belonging. Nature offers healing connections, physically and spiritually. It never says no; it always welcomes you.

I turn to nature to connect to my place and to my parents' places in the cycle of living.

Home Journal

At home I have a journal in which I wrote only about my experiences as a caregiver. I wrote in it whenever I felt like it. This journal was a place where I let it all out and, believe me, what I wrote could get pretty ugly. I harangued the doctors, my siblings, the capitalist system, and myself, showing no mercy. But between rants there occur some astonishing insights, captured moments of light, and small and simple miracles. After both my parents died, my journal was one more gift for me created through a collaboration between my parents and myself. Self-expression through writing and rereading your own words nurtures your soul.

I write about caregiving now as a release and also as a gift for myself to return to later.

Beyond Lifestyles

Chris had a very different lifestyle from that of her coworkers. Now a mail carrier on a rural route, she had lived in communes, been a political activist, and traveled extensively throughout the country. She was also gay. Most of her coworkers lived in the same town their whole lives, had married once and early, and had children. Although Chris often felt like an outsider when she became her parents' caregiver, she received enormous support from these women. They all had taken care of elderly relatives, and they shared their valuable experience with her.

Often through caregiving we encounter people in support groups, in hospital corridors, and at the work-place we otherwise wouldn't feel an urge to connect with. When outer differences give way to the deeper rhythms of life, we meet on common ground that can shatter our previous judgments about the people we only know on the surface.

One of the gifts of parentcare is the contact I make with others that goes beneath the surface of our lifestyles.

Nobody Told Me

When I find myself wishing someone had told me what to expect sooner, I remind myself that if ten years ago someone had told me I would be so involved in taking care of my parents, I wouldn't have believed them. Back then, I believed my parents would live to ripe old ages, take care of themselves until they moved into an old people's home, and quickly and peacefully die. It was what I wanted to believe and what I hoped for. Now when I hear my friends talk about their parents in this way, I know it's a stage in their development as an adult; I don't have to judge them. I can step back from convincing them of the reality without stepping away from the friendship. Hopefully when their time of parentcare comes, they'll reach out for the support that all of us need in this role.

I accept my friends wherever they are in relationship to parentcare.

Decisions, Decisions

For some people it's easy to pinpoint when they started taking care of their parents—a major event or life change propelled them into the role. For others, it's a gradual sequence of events over a period of years. Wherever you are in this spectrum, you'll eventually be making many of the decisions for the people who once made decisions for you.

Often there's time to weigh options and consider the opinions of other family members. But in an emergency you have to make immediate choices. Prepare yourself in small ways: give a neighbor or friend the name and number of your parents' home and the hospital nearest them. Alert someone at your workplace of your position as the primary caregiver so an unforeseen absence isn't totally unexpected. By taking a few steps now you'll have more focus for the unforeseen.

In small ways I prepare for unforeseen situations.

Timeless Journey

I was listening to a woman whose mother had died five years ago tell me a story about an incident between them. As she spoke of it her eyes widened and her voice dropped to a whisper. It was as if she were experiencing the exchange with her mother now. After she finished her tale and took a deep breath, she told me that it wasn't until a year ago that the exchange with her mother shed light on her own relationship with her son.

Though the tasks of parentcare end, the experiences, the emotions, and the insights they invoke remain with us to learn from later.

Even if I'm not getting the insights from parentcare now, they will unfold in the future.

Motivation in Action

Sometimes we think like this: if I don't mention to the doctor my mother's memory lapse or the fall she took the past week, then maybe she can live at home a little longer. Or, I better wait until the right moment to bring up to my parents the subject of scheduling a meeting with the lawyer. The mind likes to believe the universe is under its control even when this view leads to unfortunate physical and financial consequences. But the mind can't assuage our fears or control circumstances by putting off confronting them.

I turn inaction into action by circumventing my mind and leaning toward faith rather than fear.

New Frontiers

Eventually, you will have to limit your parent's in-dependence: take away the car, have the bills sent to you, etc. For the sake of his or her safety and your peace of mind, this situation offers few compromises. You may feel panic, dread, fear, or even anger at the thought of imposing limits on a parent. It challenges the very core of your relationship with him or her. You aren't just questioning your parent's authority like a rebellious adolescent, you're usurping it. But because you must take these steps to protect your parent, you also experience what it is like to have to change your *modus operandi* to fit in the world differently. So when you introduce new boundaries, no matter how awful it feels, draw empathy from your own discomfort and compassion for both your parent and yourself.

I draw from my strength and compassion on the in-breath and I release it into this new frontier on the out-breath.

Trampling the Flower

What do you do when your best intentions are undermined?

When my mother complained that she didn't get out enough, I planned a trip to the mall. I picked the one with her favorite makeup counter, imagining we would both have make-overs and eat lunch. When I arrived at her door, my mother was still in her housecoat. She said she was tired and her stomach was upset. I tried to spark some enthusiasm in her by relating my plans for our day. It didn't work. She asked me to go pick up some stomach medication for her and a television guide. When I returned she wanted to watch television. After tea and toast, she announced she was taking a nap. I was infuriated and at a loss. I lay down on the couch and stared at the ceiling for a while. Then I had an idea.

When my mother woke up, we sat on her porch. I told her one of my favorite anecdotes about her from my childhood. She responded in turn with a story about me. We went back and forth telling family stories for about an hour. In that time her face transformed more profoundly than a make-over could have accomplished.

Flexibility is the foundation of spiritual growth.

 *Today I am not my expectations. I'm flexible and supple.*

Sidestepping

"**D**o you think I'm an idiot? I know what's going on!"

Just because parents are old and also may have dementia doesn't mean that they don't understand what's happening around them.

You may experience the urge to protect their feelings, or you may simply want to avoid conflicts and emotional scenes with them. Whatever your reasons, speaking in whispers or withholding information about their health, care, finances, and other family problems are tactics that often fail and can provoke their anger.

Your parents have their own methods for coping with matters that are too much for them and they will use them if they're feeling overwhelmed. It's also likely that your parents know you well enough to sense when something is up. The anxiety that they develop imagining the worst can be more stressful than the truth. Don't forget, too, when you keep your parents informed, you send the message that they still are vital members of the family and that intimation makes most people feel strong.

I treat my parent with the same respect I expect for myself.

Life Expectancy

Caregiving is not only immediate crisis or temporary measures; it may be a long-term experience. People who live to the age of seventy-five have a good chance of living ten to fifteen more years, especially women. You have no control over the length of your parent's life, your own, or anybody else's.

Few circumstances are as compelling as parentcaring to motivate you to treat each day as if it were the only one you could count on. Many people consider this a morbid or frightening way to live. In truth, it's the state in which we all live every day, only we try not to think about it.

To embrace the unpredictable nature of death doesn't mean you have to be "good" at every moment because it might be your last or your parent's last. It means to acknowledge the lifetime lived in each day. If you were to silently wish your parents a final farewell each time you parted or hung up the telephone, over the months and years, such wishes would transform your relationship not only with your parents but with other loved ones.

Today I experience the lifetime contained in this day.

Interdependence

My father was always meticulous about his appearance; although I didn't share his love of plaid, I understood his pride in being a well-groomed man. Ever since I was a young boy, he stood in front of the same mirror every morning and shaved at 7:10. The first day I had to shave him shook me up, not only because it was the end of an era and another sign of his deterioration, but also because of my father's willingness to let me. Shaving my father provided us with a moment of intimacy, the depth of which I'd never experienced with him before.

There are many "first times" when caregiving. As your parent's abilities diminish, you can grow into a fuller understanding of human interdependence.

My parent's interdependence allows me to acknowledge, accept, and celebrate my own.

Proving Ground

You may be raising your own family and/or you may be successful in your career and your parents still don't trust you to make good decisions regarding their lives or your own. Is there something you want from your parents? If so, you may be relying on them emotionally, which, in turn, causes them to experience you as dependent on them! The combination of your desires—to be recognized by your mother and father, to be a loving son or daughter, to care for them, and to feel secure about your choices and dependability—can be in conflict.

Caring isn't a means of getting what you want. As a caregiver, your job isn't to prove your capabilities to your parents. The gifts of caregiving rarely resemble what you long for, but they will encompass much of what you need to learn at this point in your life.

🎁 *For today I have nothing to prove.*

Money Matters

This may be the first time you're privy to the details of your parents' finances. It can feel like an intrusion to you and to them. Your parents may want a lot of help or simply want your input during casual discussion. Assessing their resources for a limited and potentially expensive future is an emotional experience for all concerned. Tread lightly. A financial counselor will reduce the strain only if all of you are comfortable discussing money with a third party.

Each family has its particular values and rules regarding money. At the daily level, you may have to ask your parents to reimburse you for the groceries you purchase for them, or they may be slipping you twenty-dollar bills every time you turn around. Your parents may place a higher priority on leaving an inheritance than on self-care, or vice versa. You may not agree with their decision. It's a big step in letting go to honor wishes you're opposed to.

The management of your parents' financial resources also confronts you with your relationship with money in the practical, symbolic, and spiritual realms.

Whatever the outcome, slowly but surely I learn about my own relationship with money through gently and steadily assisting my parents with managing their finances.

Peeling Apples

When my great-grandfather was in his nineties, he spent his days sitting on the porch peeling apples: one long, unbroken, perfect spiral per apple. Being productive is such a part of our nature that even simple tasks are important to our sense of self-worth. For whatever the reasons, human beings are human doings also. As a busy, able-bodied person, it is easy to take for granted the basic urge to do: clean the sink, feed the cat, mark off a day on the calendar, wait for the mail to arrive, or fill out a sweepstakes form. These actions gain importance if they are the only chores a person can perform.

Rather than being annoyed by your parent's insistence on his or her daily rituals, you can appreciate his or her tenacity and creativity in finding ways to stay connected to the everyday workings of life.

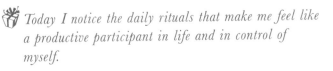

Today I notice the daily rituals that make me feel like a productive participant in life and in control of myself.

Religion

Churches, synagogues, and mosques are resources for support of parentcare. Even if you reject your parent's religious beliefs, places of worship offer social events, counseling services, and some home care for the elderly. They also house the seeds of your earliest relationship to spirituality.

Visiting the site where your religious beliefs began, whether you agree with them now or not, with your parent is one way to touch your spiritual union. When I attend services with my mother, regardless of our differing beliefs, we create a space in which we recognize each other as equal members of a holy human family.

I visit the beginnings of my spiritual life as a step into my new relationship with my parents.

Which Family?

Your son is having a hard time in school, your spouse feels abandoned, and you've spent your vacation money on parentcare. You don't want to neglect your family, but which family? You feel divided between two: the one you came from and the one you've created. How can it be that you have to choose?

You don't have to, not in the ultimate sense.

When you first fell in love, you wanted to be everything for your beloved. After a time you realized that no matter what you did or said, your beloved had needs beyond you. When you have a baby, you also want to care for and protect your child in every way; in fact, this is your job. But there are days and nights when no matter what you do, you can't console your baby.

You can't do everything for your parents, either. Love doesn't mean doing it all for *anyone*.

You have to integrate parentcare into the family life you've established. Often it requires making adjustments within your family—adjustments, not sweeping reform. The best any of us can do is to try to determine what needs are most important to each member of both families, and then to reorganize the playing field so that most of the time most of your family is getting most of what's most important to them—including you.

I move beyond all-or-nothing thinking about the family I came from and the family I've created.

Vestments

In simple actions are great lessons. For months I battled with my mother about getting dressed. I became anxious, frustrated, and short-tempered waiting for her. In turn, she, too, became anxious and frustrated. Finally, I decided that if she couldn't move more swiftly, I would take over.

The first morning I went to her closet to take out a dress. When I peered at the rack of hanging garments, I suddenly saw all the decisions and choices involved in the simple act of dressing. As I knelt before my mother to help her with her stockings, I saw her once again as more than the sum of her abilities, and I felt pretty foolish for not recognizing this sooner. Then I realized that I, too, was more than the list of my abilities. From that morning on, dressing my mother, once a source of contention, became a daily meditation for both of us.

Parent, child, beloved, sibling, or friend, we are more than the sum of our abilities.

It Goes with You

As caregivers when our parents' needs increase, we come to know their habits to a tee. A new component is added to our psyche—constant vigilance about their well-being. Our concern and feelings of responsibility are never far from the surface. They take a toll. They follow us everywhere: to work, the gym, the movie lobby, after making love in the Bahamas, and before breakfast. Being new, they're quite obvious at first. But after a time our hyperawareness and concern weaves into the fabric of our life. Or does it?

Even when we aren't consciously aware of how our energies are being sapped by concern, it can pull us off balance and set us up for a fall. Yet sometimes the more we try to escape from a thought pattern, the more predominant it becomes.

I accept the concerned voice that speaks up just when I'm having fun, and then I return to the joy that I need to keep up my strength.

Ask

What have you always wondered about your parent? You know some of her history, but are there periods about which you have questions? Perhaps there are family events on which her perspective is unclear to you.

To ask is to knock on the door. It's a sign of respect. It lets her know you are present, that you wish to gain entry. Like knocking, asking is an invitation: are you ready to let me in? It isn't a guarantee of an open door or an answer. But as people come closer to the finite nature of their life span, they're often more willing to share thoughts and anecdotes about themselves and others.

Now is the time to collect your questions. Write them down, and over the next few days, months, or years, ask. You won't have the opportunity forever.

Don't be put off if her reply is brief or curt or she says nothing at all; through asking, the answers to your questions will be as much in her eyes and in her body as in her words.

I ask questions and recognize the answers in all their forms.

Family Affair

I tried keeping all my siblings abreast of every detail of what I was doing for our father. They would nod in agreement to all of it, but they never would make decisions or offer opinions. Then they'd talk about my decisions among themselves but never directly to me. My expectation was that they would be helpful and participate. The reality was that they each had methods of participation that didn't fit my ideas of how a family should operate. I had to learn to take actions without informing them *ad nauseam*.

My expectations were the way I tried to control the situation. When I stepped back and accepted my family's and my own limits, life became easier, and oddly enough my siblings became more helpful.

I can temper my expectations of my family by recognizing the importance of every person.

Number Two: A Quiz

Does the moaning and groaning from the bathroom drive you up a wall? Who wants to know their parent's toilet schedule? Is the fact that your parent's excrement is something you have to clean up giving you the heebie-jeebies? Do your parents talk about their bowel movements with the interest of new parents conversing about their baby's poop?

Nature is as raw as it is complex. What is normal in life shifts regularly. For instance, once your bodily functions were a legitimate concern to your parents. Your natural body functions were no less worthy of attention than a snowflake or a cactus.

As I allow "normal" to evolve, I make room for the raw.

Lost

Perhaps you're feeling lost—each of you—aging parent and caregiver offspring. You're in new terrain and trying to find your way. You're wandering on parallel tracts—one, the way of finishing out this life; the other, the way of approaching the role of an elder.

Remember what it was like to be lost when you were a child? Panicked and disoriented, you searched for something familiar. You needed reassurance from yourself and sometimes from strangers. You probably got lost by leaving the security of the known, letting your appetite for new horizons take a front seat to your fear of the unknown.

This is how most growth, progress, and insight is attained. When you finally regained your bearings, you may not always have liked where you found yourself, but you probably gained precious gifts during the journey.

With empathy, I reassure myself and my parents, and I take in reassurance from others as we wander the unknown together.

Dance

At my brother's wedding reception my father led the rumba line. He was beaming, the old gray fox, stepping and shaking at seventy-plus. His body movements were infused with the wisdom of joy. Later on in the festivities I slow-danced with an elderly great-aunt. Holding her hand and waist as we waltzed, I experienced the essence of time flowing through her.

Dance with your parents, even if one of them is wheelchair-bound or confined to bed. Turn on the music, hold her hand, and dance with age. Let go of thoughts. Without words, allow the life force to flicker between you.

Today I dance with age and follow its lead.

Bureaucratic Oaths

Eventually, you may become responsible for overseeing your parent's affairs. It is overwhelming to be called on suddenly to understand and to act on such issues as securing Medicare, protecting assets, setting up living trusts and powers of attorney, and negotiating health care, not to mention finding the time to do it all. These new responsibilities can make you feel inept and more and more frustrated with each telephone call when you are put on hold. The injustice of seemingly arbitrary rules can nudge your own authority issues into full-bloomed craziness. You know you're not the first person to go through this, so why is it so hard?

Go ahead, throw a tantrum. It may be necessary to go through angry tears before you can accept reality: no one is out to get you, it isn't personal, it's just the way it is.

After I passed through feelings of victimization by the system, I was able to ask for help. Then things fell into place. Through a local Alzheimer's organization, I was referred to a lawyer who specializes in eldercare issues. She led me to the best adult day care center in my state.

Today I take a deep breath, remember that others have gone before me, and call on someone for help.

Photographs

I took many pictures of my father during his last years. In part, I wanted to hold on to him in any way I could. I also recall thinking, He won't be the same next month, I need a way to remember him. I compared my last photographs of him with those in the family album that depicted the fiery, young, passionate, and muscular father of my memory. I realized that with my final snapshots of him, I was trying to locate his dwindling life force through the camera lens. I found it, too, but in subtler places: the way he squared his shoulders as he posed, his smirk, and then looking beyond the photographs—in aspects of myself.

Today I focus less with my eyes and more with my heart.

Beauty and the Beast

We have an atrophied idea of beauty. We say a rose is more beautiful than a beetle, confusing personal preference with the essence and the intelligence of what's around us. Giving more credence to an aesthetic over the authentic confines us and deprives us of essential nourishment. Living under the vigorous youth model of beauty limits how elders see themselves and how we see them. We have to consciously shake the glitter from our eyes. It blinds us to the cycles of our life and the gifts that each one gives us. We sacrifice ourselves to an idol by placing a higher value on harmony divorced from truth. Truth is the first beauty from which all aesthetic is born. There's an intelligence to everything in nature, including the way we age. Now look at your elder parents and see their beauty.

I find the beauty in reality and nourish myself from the cycles of life.

"You're Just Like Your Mother"

Time and again you're told how you're just like one of your parents. From your third cousin to your siblings and spouse, you can practically sense it coming. During certain periods of your life this is an insult, stealing your sense of identity and self-determination. Now as your relationship with your parents intensifies, the ways you're alike are a point of reference. They're where empathy in earnest begins.

When accepting the similarities as they surface over the period of caregiving, you slowly will come to understand that when you're tending to your obstinate mother or your shy father, you're also learning new ways to care for those aspects of yourself. You are, on one level, a combination of your mother and your father. When you care for them, you are, on many levels, caring for yourself as well.

I learn new levels of caring for myself as I care for my parents.

The Eye of the Beholder

Children, no matter what their age, want the approval of their parents. At one point I began bringing flowers to my mother to improve the atmosphere of the house a little bit. She never mentioned them. I was disappointed and complained to a friend. He wondered out loud if it was the beauty of the flowers or the beauty of my love that I wanted my mother to acknowledge. A few days later as I fumbled for my keys to my mother's house, I glanced through the glass in the door and noticed her sprucing up the bouquet on the coffee table.

I trust that my parents appreciate my love even if they don't always show it.

Breaking Bread

Eating meals together was when I had some of the closest moments with my dad. He'd pass the bread, I'd pour him a glass of his favorite soda; literally and figuratively, we nourished each other. Every religion has rituals in which food is a symbol that links us to the past and to the spiritual realm. The simplicity of a shared meal sometimes can establish more harmony than a planned family discussion. Without the television on to distract us, or a newspaper to hide behind, our meals together were a kind of meditation on love. After a time we ate more slowly and deliberately, and the awkward silences stopped feeling awkward and more like pockets of tranquillity. Even some of my father's eating habits that once drove me to cringe became practically poetic.

Today I share a meal with my parents as a meditation. Whatever insights I draw, I apply to my role in their care.

One Emotion, Many Faces

Everyone who practices parentcare experiences anger. It has many faces: jealousy toward your friends whose parents enjoy good health or better fortune; self-blame; a feeling that people around you are insensitive; a belief that nobody understands how upset you are or how bad the situation is. Anger likes a target so you may find someone to blame. A doctor, social worker, or family member is the most common mark. In the same way, everyone who lives to be an aging parent experiences anger through a corresponding spectrum. The more familiar you become with the faces of anger that you and your parents wear, the more respectfully and nimbly you can detach from anger's grasp.

If I sense anger today, I will name its face.

Common Sense

A lot of parentcare is common sense. But common sense can be elusive when big emotions and fears cloud your thinking. When there's no picture on your mother's television, take a deep breath and do the simplest thing first: check to see if the set is plugged in. When you feel overwhelmed by the upcoming day of looking at care facilities with your parents, do what's in front of you first: eat a good breakfast, shake hands with the facility manager, take your mother's arm as you tour the grounds.

At every moment your common sense is with you. You access it by becoming as simple as possible. Then the storm of emotions and impressions your mind is kicking up will subside. The immediate next step will be clear. It will be a very small step. Small steps are good; they don't tire you out too quickly.

Today I breathe deeply to retrieve my common sense; I take small steps.

Body Double

In the examination room we waited for the doctor. My father took off his clothes, got on the table, and partially covered his body with a sheet. We were awkward and silent. I looked around the room for something to distract me. When that failed, I gazed at my father. Like a glow, I saw his young body emanating from the older body. Just as suddenly, he looked seventy again as if nothing had happened. For that moment I thought I might have witnessed the essence of his life force. But where was it coming from? Him? Me?

I accept unusual visions that may occur as interesting possibilities that enrich my soul.

Negative Support Systems

We are surrounded by negativity. It takes conscious effort to fight it. Write down your gloomy concepts of old people and then beside each one write an experience that disproves it.

The most destructive support you must curtail, however, is that from others. You may know people—within or outside of your family—who cultivate their negativity and, by your association with them, yours as well. These folks get a high from martyrdom, collect sympathy from self-pity, or get attention railing against "the system." While we each need to vent our frustrations, and we all can benefit from taking some civic action related to eldercare, some people make a hobby of complaining out of self-righteousness and fear of true change.

You'll recognize these quashing supporters when they try to sabotage your new relationship to eldercare. "Get real," they'll say when what they mean is, don't veer from *their* reality. Their comments aren't concern; they are an attack on your judgment and self-esteem.

Detach yourself from these people. You can't change them. Be firm. Trust the new relationship you're developing with your parents and with yourself. If it isn't enough, you can always go back to bemoaning anytime.

I actively protect myself from negative support systems.

The Long and Winding Road

Parentcare is a long haul. Like giving birth or long-distance running, you have to pace yourself. In relation to caregiving, this action means trading off responsibilities every now and then with your eldercare team. It means choosing your battles. It means remembering that at one level, life is a series of negotiations. It also means embracing ironies: slowing down sometimes gets you where you're going faster; you must get serious about lightening up.

Today I take the long view of parentcare and adjust my expectations of others and of myself.

Beck and Call

Do you expect your parents to be available at your beck and call just because you're caring for them? You have a busy life that is pulling you in many directions. But consider what it's like to need help and have little or no input about its availability. Of course, it isn't practical to fit your own life around your parents' schedule, either.

Meet them partway. Call ahead before any visit, even if your parents insist you don't have to call first. If you make appointments for them, be mindful of the meetings they attend or the television shows they like; if there's a conflict, be sure to acknowledge it and apologize for the inconvenience. These courtesies are a message to your parents that you view their time as valuable, too. It also means that you've progressed beyond the childlike expectation that your parents are available on demand.

Today I respect time.

Careful

One afternoon I was eating lunch with my father. He kept repeating his plans to clean out the bird cage and separate the plastic from the glass and cans for recycling. By then I knew his mentioning something several times helped him to remember it, but this day he seemed nervous, almost agitated.

After clearing the dishes, we sat in the living room and my father dozed off in his favorite chair. Quietly, I cleaned out the bird cage and sorted the recycling while he slept. When he woke up, like a proud child, I showed him what I'd done. His face fell. He wouldn't look at me. He turned on the television without a word. He didn't answer his telephone for the rest of the day. At the time I didn't understand that in my haste to care for my father, I'd robbed him of the chores that made him feel capable and useful.

Today I will be careful to not overstep the boundaries of caregiving.

Inner Elder

Caring for your elderly parents presents opportunities to connect to the elder within you. It's the part of you that's wiser than your years, that's earned you your gray hairs. The youth-oriented hype of our culture constantly denigrates old age, demanding that you hide signs of aging on penalty of being ignored and left out. It's easy to get caught in denying your inner elder in the midst of hiding the outward signs of aging. As you care for your parents, it is also your chance to access the store of wisdom that resides within you.

Today I listen for the wisdom of my inner elder. I invite this aspect of myself to come forward.

Sore Spots

One of the reasons people dread parentcare is that the process constantly touches off our emotional tender spots. We normally avoid situations that bring us up against our insecurity, shame, perfectionism, jealousy, etc. While it's natural to evade circumstances that cause pain and put us in direct contact with our weaknesses, it isn't always the best choice. That is, you can prevent growth by protecting yourself from yourself. When you shy away from your parents because in their company your sore spots hurt, you're pointing the finger at the messenger rather than the message. (There may be periods of your life when you benefit from a time-out from your parents, but for most of us, the benefit is lost if the separation is permanent.)

Every week you care for your parents, situations arise that expose you to your tender places. Each time is an opportunity to heal the sore place by accepting yourself, forgiving yourself your imperfections, and staying open to another way of being. To move beyond your sore spots, you must move through them.

When I come up against a sore spot, I separate the messenger from the message.

Avoidance

It became unsafe for my father to drive anymore. I dreaded confronting him directly with this situation. In fact, at first I avoided it by devising schemes. My first ploy was to take his car keys: the primary and spare sets. The car sat in the driveway for a couple of days. On day three, the car was gone and so was Dad. Always prepared, he had a third set. My second tactic was to wait until he was busy in the backyard and then loosen the distributor cap. I was sure this would render the car unstartable. I'd have it towed to the shop and tell him it couldn't be fixed. The next morning, the driveway was empty and down the road I saw the car coughing and backfiring but still running on three of its eight cylinders. That's when I knew that I couldn't avoid what I had to do. When he pulled into the driveway, I gently took the keys from his hand and said, "Dad, I'm sorry I have to tell you this, but you can't drive anymore." I took a deep breath and prepared myself to encounter my biggest fear—my father's anger.

Trickery is only a temporary measure.

Getting the Job

This is a powerful time in your life. You've earned the position to care not only for yourself but for the others before and after you. How did you qualify? Perhaps through your compassion, your sense of humor, your previous experience, or your organizational skills. Perhaps you got the job because of your potential.

Like with any new job, you will need time to learn how to do it well. Along the way you'll be promoted. Your responsibilities will increase. You'll get along with some of your coworkers better than with others. You may be subject to evaluations of your performance. What are the benefits? They vary from family to family, but they always include vacation and sick days and an incredible personal growth package.

Today I meet my new position with confidence instead of perfectionism.

In Partnership with Professionals

Caring for parents is a collaboration. From the lawyer's secretary to the medical specialists, I found a mix of caring individuals who were enthusiastic about their professions, and indifferent people who were burned out or untrained in eldercare issues.

I became flexible and cooperative: polite, patient, but also persistent when I needed to be. No matter who it was, I kept in mind that we were establishing a relationship, and I wanted it to be as supportive of my parents as possible.

First, I adjusted my expectations. Health professionals often maintain emotional distance from their clients to ensure as care providers that they don't become drained. Because they service so many people, their time is also limited. So when one of the doctors spent two hours with my mother, I was thrilled, but I didn't expect it from everyone. I wrote down my questions before appointments. I learned to ask people to explain in another way what I didn't understand. If I was truly uncomfortable with one member of the team we'd assembled, I found a replacement.

Every partnership involves a realistic view of each member's strengths and shortfalls, a willingness to compensate for them, and shared risks and responsibilities.

I establish partnerships with professionals.

Toe to Toe

The days and weeks that followed my taking my father's car from him were some of the most difficult. He tried to convince the police to arrest me. Whenever I went to see him, he began screaming at me as soon as I walked through the door, furious over what I had done. He left me nasty messages on my answering machine. It was awful—just what I had feared most about unleashing his wrath. I also knew I was absolutely right about taking away his car. It simply wasn't safe for him to drive. I knew his anger wasn't really at me but at not being able to drive. Still I had to endure it. As terrible as it felt, it also was transformative to stand there taking on my father's fury, toe to toe, and still be direct and unyielding: *I hear your anger. I understand it, but you cannot drive.* I repeated this over and over during these days and weeks. It became a mantra for me. Eventually, his rage ran its course and our relationship came back into balance. I actually experienced a greater closeness to him and I was able to be more direct and honest with him from then on. It was a good reminder about standing firm in my convictions.

I can withstand fury when my actions come firmly from a caring place.

Comparing Notes

Caring for your parents doesn't mean doing everything for them. We each contribute what we can. Your friend who quit her job and moved in with her parents isn't a better caregiver than you are just because she's devoting more time to her folks.

Parentcare *does* require that you stretch your limits. That's why it's an experience from which you grow and develop as a person. But care and growth aren't always measured by a time clock.

No one can tell you what is or is not enough time and energy to devote to parentcare. And whatever amount of time you allot, it will change as new circumstances develop.

You don't have to compare yourself with others. You don't have to keep up—not even with your parents' expectations of you. You have to do the best you can and grow to trust your intuition.

I trust my own ability to care for my parents and myself.

Laugh Out Loud

Laughter heals. It's good for you and your parents. It's even better when you do it together. Laughter releases tension and stress. It may not be simple to meet your parents in laughter. Your father's humor may be *The Three Stooges* while yours is *Seinfeld*.

My own mother couldn't stand her father's puns. But occasionally he delivered one she grudgingly admired. When she was able to let him see her appreciation for a moment, they both became noticeably more supple and at ease. It was marvelous to see.

Laughing at yourself is also a vital part of parent-care. It cures you. Of what? It cures you of taking yourself too seriously. Start with some irony, like when you rush to leave town for a weekend away from your folks and you end up driving behind an elderly couple going well below the speed limit on a one-lane road. Then try a little exaggeration. Imagine an overblown version of your style of caregiving as if you were a character in a situation comedy: the idealistic daughter whose everything-is-beautiful attitude drives her old folks batty, or the computer whiz who develops an eldercare software program for meals, medications, and exercise and expects his parents to abide by it. If all else fails, have someone tickle you.

I find something to laugh about today; maybe even myself.

Inside/Outside

Ian's practice included an office for Marvin, his seventy-nine-year-old, semiretired father. One afternoon after the patients had left, Ian walked into his father's office and found Marvin balanced on a chair he had hoisted onto his desk to change a light bulb. Caught, using the same authoritative voice he used when Ian was a young boy, Marvin said, "Go to the waiting room, right now!"

Ian was so taken aback by the combination of that old tone of voice and seeing his father perched so precariously that he did what he was told. A few minutes later, Marvin joined his son and explained.

"I know you think I'm foolish to be doing such a thing, but I forget. I don't feel seventy-nine; I feel thirty-five. Sometimes when I look in the mirror I get a shock: who is that old guy? My inside and my outside don't match."

Ian nodded. He understood; he was in his forties, and he didn't feel a day over thirty himself. How old do you feel inside?

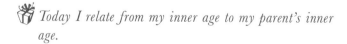 *Today I relate from my inner age to my parent's inner age.*

Generation Gap

The majority of our parents would never have thought to read a book like this. Their generation grew up with different ways of coping. Generally speaking, one parent would keep his feelings behind the newspaper and the other would make everything all right. But our folks seeded our ability to be different from them. How? Part of the answer is between the lines of what they say, and another part is stored in their bodies, surfacing in the way they go about their daily activities. As a caregiver you are in a rare position to observe the more subtle origins of your individuality.

 Taking into consideration our generational differences, I look at how my parents helped to shape the person I am.

A Fable

A long time ago, in a faraway place, a traveler came upon a village tucked away in a dale. At the entry to the village were two statues built out of mud and sticks. One was of an old man and the other an old woman. When the traveler looked on these dried-up, bony figures, he chuckled: what kind of people try to scare outsiders with these old mud piles? It was about an hour before sunset and the villagers were busy ending their day's work. They ignored the traveler's questions concerning the mud-and-stick statues, where he could get a bite to eat, and where he could sleep the night. Their only reply was, "Sir, each minute is precious, and praise be to you for lending a hand." He was insulted by their strange reply, and he had no notion how he was lending a hand. He set about to get his revenge and show these ignorant villagers a thing or two. As night fell, he tore down the mud statues. His fury grew with each handful of dirty sticks he threw away. After dismantling the figures, he staggered into the village square, lay down exhausted, and fell asleep.

In the morning the village baker and the village grocer politely greeted the traveler and served him breakfast. Their hospitality confused the traveler even more. Hadn't they noticed what he had done? Why weren't they scared of him? No one seemed the slightest bit concerned when he boasted that he had torn apart the old muddy crones. And when he pointed in their direction, he saw the statues were still standing.

From the vernal equinox to the autumnal equinox, he tore down the statues every night, collapsing in the square afterward, only to awake to their reappearance. Finally, he was too exhausted to tear them down again, and as the sun set, he fell asleep right there at their feet. That night he dreamt of a large pool of water surrounded by an embankment of mud and sticks, and when he gazed into the pool he saw an old man staring back at him. When he awoke he went to the fountain in the square, looked at his reflection, and saw that it was no dream.

No matter how hard you resist your own impending journey toward old age, your time will come.

I look for my personal fable in my relationship to parentcare.

Revenge

During parentcare, if you find yourself in a position to assert power over your parents, you might be struck by an urge to get back at them for the ways they've hurt you, especially if they were abusive or neglectful. You may have even fantasized about how you'd do it. Sometimes people unconsciously act out their desire for revenge by forgetting to do things for their parents. If you have the urge to settle the score, or you have a history with your parents that would give you cause to want revenge, it's important to recognize two things. First, it isn't so uncommon a feeling as you may imagine. It's natural to want to retaliate when you've been wronged. The *feeling* is normal and probably healthy. It's *acting* on the feeling that leads to unbearable guilt later on.

Second, revenge is a desire that is best not to underestimate. In literature and cinema it's a recurring motivation in countless classic and modern tragedies. Therefore, it's important to discuss your feelings with someone you trust and who has experience with parentcare and the urge for revenge, so that you can arrive at a way to manage your urges, your fantasies, and parentcare.

I share with others the source of my desire for revenge rather than acting on it.

Wandering

After we had to take my father's car from him, he started going for walks. It seemed like a good idea to us. It was mild exercise, everyone in the neighborhood knew him, and he lived in a safe part of town. Our family even agreed that walking was much healthier for him than driving.

One Saturday my brother called me to see if Dad was ready to go shopping. I had stopped by my father's house earlier and when I saw he wasn't home, I thought he and my brother had already left.

After two hours of frantic searching, we decided to call the police. As we approached Dad's house to make the call, he was walking up the driveway. Dad insisted he had taken a short walk, but he looked exhausted and worn. We figured he'd walked for three hours. We learned a lesson and through it developed a different strategy for his care.

The urge to berate myself and go over the possibilities of what could have happened to my father was powerful. My brother and I needed each other to remind ourselves to be grateful nothing awful took place and to concentrate on creating a new plan of action.

No one can possibly protect another person at every moment. It is enough to do my best.

"Take Care of Me"

Just as certain people cling to their independence as they age, many become extremely dependent. After her husband's death, Bill's mother wanted him to do everything from taking out the garbage to balancing her checkbook. It was painful for Bill to set limits, but without them his mother would have given up on and given away her life.

Some people also value and hold fast to their independence regarding the activities of their daily life but nevertheless become deeply and often unconsciously emotionally dependent on you. If one of your parents fits this description, his emotional neediness may seem to come out of nowhere. He may not be able to express his emotional needs directly to you. He may send you a lot of mixed messages: don't take care of me/take care of me; leave me alone/you never call; you're impossible/you care about me. You'll have to experiment with creating a balance between pointing out his contradictions, clarifying his needs, and taking the role of detective—deciphering his coded messages.

As you learn what your parents need and want from you, you'll have to decide what you can and cannot give. There's no formula for this. Your intuition is your guide.

Today I'm alert for the line between caring for my parents and enabling them to give up responsibility for their lives.

Wrinkles in Time

The pervasive obsession with maintaining a youthful appearance is the antithesis of the spirit of discovery; it stems from *not* wanting to look where we're going rather than enthusiastically exploring the unknown. The wrinkles on your parent's face are a map. It isn't really that wrinkles are ugly, it's that we associate them with death.

Yet we prefer aged wines, we find the oldest trees the most majestic, we travel great distances to be in the presence of ancient ruins, and we covet antique furniture. We revere age everywhere else and at the same time attempt to deny it in ourselves.

Study the wrinkles on your parent's face. Scrutinize them. Some are from laughter and smiles and others are from worry and hardship. Like any map, they're proof of a journey. As your parent's journey comes to a close, those wrinkles are calling to you to decipher them like a treasure map so that you can get your bearings.

I study the wrinkles on my parent's face. From them I create a map of the intersecting moments of our lives; I use it to get my bearings.

Journals

I wrote a lot during my years of parentcare. I needed extraordinary means for coping with my parents' needs and my own emotions. I carried a small brown notebook with me. Sometimes when my mother was venting her anger, I would sit at the kitchen table and write down verbatim what she was saying. It probably looked ridiculous: her screaming while I furiously jotted down notes like some journalist with a hot news story. But the act of writing took the edge off of my emotional depletion.

Sometimes all you can do is get through the moment. Writing is a way to release and encapsulate feelings.

Today I use another tool I have to help my caregiving.

The Riddle of the Sphinx

From Greek mythology comes the riddle of the Sphinx: what starts off in the morning walking on four legs, walks on two in the afternoon, and three in the evening? The answer is us. Embedded in this riddle is the understanding of an important aspect of aging. In the morning and afternoon—or infancy and adulthood—we move on that with which we were born; crawling or walking, we get around on our own steam. But at night—in old age—our third "leg" is symbolized by a cane.

The cane represents external support. We don't come ready-made with canes. They're created—by human handiwork. The riddle demonstrates how, through the ages, it's expected that we receive help in our later years.

You are part of your parent's cane. Along with siblings, medical professionals, social workers, and lawyers, your care contributes to your parent's third leg. When you telephone daily, do the grocery shopping, arrange for day care, or all of these things, you're strengthening your parent's cane. You also demonstrate to those around you how they can assist you in the evening of your life.

Today I stand on my two feet and lend a helping hand.

Time Travelers

Once while we were doing dishes, I asked my father in passing when he'd last spoken to his younger sister, Belva. At the mention of her name he went into a tirade: she got the dance classes, he had to work instead of going to college, she didn't help take care of their mother until the very end and that was only so Belva could collect the insurance. I felt like a time traveler. As he spoke, he kept switching back and forth between the past and the present tense. It was the first time he revealed his bitter resentment and jealousy toward his sister to me. The only time my father had even hinted at it was through an occasional joke about her always getting the attention when they were children.

Over the next months and years, I witnessed my father's return to many former loves, hates, and dreams. It could happen at any time. From touching and compassionate to ugly and painful, suppressed or muted aspects of my father emerged. Each time he revealed more about himself, and often these episodes gave me greater insight about aspects of myself. Because my father was a fairly private person, I had few other means to gain access to these levels of him.

When I follow my parent into his or her past, I return to the present enlightened.

Who Are They?

What makes an individual? Our analytical brain can break us down and sort us into our abilities, our emotions, and our accomplishments, as well as other categories. But which, if any, makes us who we are?

As your parents' abilities diminish, their emotions become more erratic, and as their accomplishments recede into the past, you may find yourself feeling they aren't themselves anymore. What do you really mean? We are more than the sum of our parts. Our spirit permeates aspects of our character, but that spirit isn't confined to them.

As an experiment, make a list of the people in your life who have died. Beside each name write down one idea that captures the person's spirit as it now resides in your consciousness. My grandfather is a wizard, Ida is an ox, Leslie is squeezed, and Michael is an electrical buzz. Your parents also have an essence. It's who they are now, later, and after they die.

I open to recognizing the essences of my parents beyond the sum of their parts.

Pioneers Muddling Through the Day

Not only are you in a quandary about how to manage parentcare, but your society as a whole shares the same dilemma. As for your parents, it's the first time they've been this old, so they, too, are trying to figure out what they need. You're pioneers in eldercare, on the cusp of a cultural shift. It's a good thing to remember as you muddle through the day. With a broader view, you may not be so hard on yourself and your parents. After all, everyone from the individual to the society at large is making it up as they go along.

In the light of the broader view, I cut myself some slack.

The Body Knows

The first time I had to be away, the person I lined up to take care of my mother mixed up the dates. My mother was without supervision for three days. I found her in the kitchen wearing three sweaters, two robes, and a pair of my father's old pants. The furnace had broken. I felt a swirl of emotions rising like a wave of nausea. All my plans for work that day had to be canceled. I took my mother to the doctor. I was in high gear. By the end of the day, everything was OK again.

Then the floodgates opened: my bones ached, my feet cramped, I broke into a sweat, and I cried. For about twenty minutes, I couldn't stop chattering. The whole spell lasted two hours. I slept through the night, though my dreams were full of turmoil. My body was discharging the knot of emotions and thoughts about my mother's condition in my absence. In my dreams, more of my psyche was released.

The body is wise. It knows what it needs. When I first saw my father strapped to a bed in the Intensive Care Unit, I craved a steak even though I'm a vegetarian. Sometimes you must hold your emotions in check to be effective, but later you must give your body equal time to center and unburden through exercise, voice release, or its own spontaneous cleansing methods.

I listen to and trust my body.

Healing Arts

Modern innovation has no hold on the eternal. Throughout human history the understanding of the perpetual cycle of aging into death is passed from generation to generation through the arts. In Western culture, from the paintings of Rembrandt such as *Jacob Blessing the Sons of Joseph* to the sculptures of Rodin, from the literature of Plato's time to the poems of Emily Dickinson, the arts have been a pool of reflection, renewal, and catharsis in which to bathe when you feel depleted or confused.

In the waters of a painting, a statue, or a poem, you will find company and comfort when sadness or despair has seeped into your bones. Enter a museum, visit a sculpture garden, open a book and read a poem. You don't have to know anything about art or poetry for some images and words to touch you in the deepest part of your pain and to offer you solace.

Today I refresh my spirit with art and poetry.

Labeling Drawers

You and your family may try to trick the memory loss. Labeling my father's drawers was one of my sister's methods: socks, underwear, gloves, etc.

My father kept three calendars: one in the kitchen, one in the bedroom, and another in the living room. Each morning he would mark off the day on all three, one right after the other. At first these measures seemed to work to make us all feel that we had a handle on his condition. But sometimes one day would turn into three and by the time my father read the labels on the drawers, he forgot what he was looking for.

I can't outsmart memory loss for long. If my parent creates devices to outsmart memory loss, I can remember that it is his condition and his choice how he will deal with it.

Mirages

Because you don't really have control over your parents—how they'll respond, what they'll do, the ways they're changing—it doesn't help you to give up controlling them. You have to give up your illusion that you *can* control them, or anyone else—health care professionals, family members.

We must remind ourselves all the time that although we've taken on roles and responsibilities as caregivers, no one also bestowed us with omniscience.

Our wish to control comes from a loving place; we want the best for our parents and we believe that we know what best means. If only they would listen. Believing we know best is also an illusion. Nobody *knows* best; we all *do* our best and hope for the most positive outcome.

I let go of the illusions of control and all-knowing.

Listen

B y now you've actualized some of what your parents wanted for you, and all of you to varying degrees have accepted that there are dreams you might not fulfill: you married or you didn't, you had children or you didn't, you have a career your parents approve of or you don't.

As your parents age and need your help, they develop new expectations of you that are demanding in another way. Along with assisting with the mechanics of daily life, you must remember that your parents need to be heard.

There are three ways to listen to old people. The first way is to pretend to be listening while you're thinking about or doing something else. The second way is to take the attitude that you will endure their chatter. The third way is to listen with genuine attention for the single word or phrase nestled in their talk that bears a message for you.

Sure, your parent may repeat the same thing again and again, especially if she has dementia, but aren't there a few important lessons you've only been able to learn in your life through their repetition?

Today I will listen.

Through the Eyes of a Child

My father's condition was rapidly declining when he flew to Michigan to visit my brother. In fact, it was pretty obvious that it would be his last trip to see his son. My brother tried his best to cope with his feelings about the obvious downturn in our father's condition. But it was his own son, seven-year-old Ross, who made the visit joyful and memorable. Ross treated his grandfather as an equal. The two of them went on many walks, and Ross liked hearing the same story several times. They played games without paying too much attention to the rules and had a great time together that Ross still remembers fondly.

Often children embrace where we judge. It was a gift to my brother to see our father through Ross's eyes.

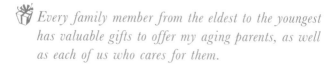

Every family member from the eldest to the youngest has valuable gifts to offer my aging parents, as well as each of us who cares for them.

Knowing the Unknown

You know that your aging parents are going to die. What you don't know is when, or how the process will affect you. But even if you did, all the knowledge in the world cannot protect you from the experience of severing these lifelong links. The unknown is out of your control: you have no shape or form to draw from, there is no goal to achieve. It is a process through which your faith and trust in others is either developed or deepened. No one passes a course called Dealing with Elderly Parents 101 and is ready to face the unknowable, but there are graduates of the living experience to help you move through the journey.

Because I do not know all the answers, I will learn to build trust with others who have gone through this journey ahead of me.

Sweetheart Days

E very Thursday, Annie drives two hours to help her mother and give her stepfather a break from caregiving. She used to be filled with anxiety: would it be a "sweetheart day" or a terrible day? On sweetheart days her mother is calm and calls Annie "sweetheart." On terrible days her mother is cantankerous. She calls Annie "stupid" and criticizes her clothes.

Frustrated and desperate, Annie bought a small tape player. She planned to record her mother on a terrible day and then play it for her on a sweetheart day in hopes that her mother, hearing how abusive she was being, would stop. But when it came to turning the tape player on, Annie felt a rush of discomfort. Trusting her instinct, she put the tape deck back in her car.

On the way home she turned it on and talked about why she wanted to confront her mother. By the time she got home, Annie felt a sense of release. The tape recorder turned out to be a great idea. She made recording her feelings a regular part of the drive home from her weekly visits. She'd discovered a way to decompress from the day and work through some feelings.

Unique ways to cope with emotions emerge if you listen to yourself and give your ideas time to evolve.

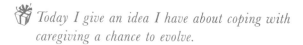 *Today I give an idea I have about coping with caregiving a chance to evolve.*

Weeding

Circumstances that merit worry abound in parent-care. In itself, worry isn't a bad emotion. It clues you in to the fact that something isn't right. What makes worry a problem is when it grows into more than a signal and turns into a state of mind.

Take steps to contain your worry because if you look back at your own history, you're sure to find that worrying over something never has helped you cope with it. In fact, it probably weakened you by taking up your energy and focus.

Our favorite techniques for containing worry are: designate a five-minute- to one-hour-per-day session devoted exclusively to worry through thinking or writing and save it all up for that session; draw yourself with your arms in the air and put one labeled ball above for each of your worries; make a list of everything you're getting out of doing and everything you're missing out on doing by using your energy to worry.

Worry is a weed. If you don't do something about it, it takes over and chokes out everything else. Parent-care challenges you to master putting your worry in check; it's good practice for placing all kinds of other limits, too.

I place limits on my worry today.

Elder Artists

Anna Mary Robertson, a.k.a. Grandma Moses, had not even started painting her lively pictures of rural life until age seventy-six, and she lived to be 101. Even with failing vision, Matisse worked into his eighties, cutting out large colored paper images for collages. The abstract expressionist Willem de Kooning continues to paint even though he lives with Alzheimer's. Much of his latest work is inviting and full of life. Looking at elder art is one way to dispel your belief that old people have little new or important to say, or that they lack creative spirit. Although your elder parents may not be artists, in their way they still have insights to offer you.

Today I'm open to the insights that my elder parents have to offer me.

Criticism

Here you are busting your buns, working with lawyers, doctors, your parents' needs—and your sister criticizes the job you are doing. Angry, hurt, and insulted, you don't call her for three weeks. You know from long experience the limitations and obstructions that exist in your family. In many families criticism is the *modus operandi* for coping with an array of uncomfortable emotions. If family members always have been critical, then they will continue to be through parentcare. If it's a new element in your family dynamic, it might be worthwhile to discuss it.

Criticism can sting. It makes some people feel electrocuted. It can cause you to question yourself. It helps to get some distance from the remark. Write it down but as an option instead of an accusation: *You* could've *been more assertive with the nurse* instead of *You* should've *been more assertive with the nurse*. Put the paper away. In this way you can separate the remark from the person who made it. (If you find the papers piling up because of one person, you may want to put some space between the two of you.) When you feel ready, review the remark. As you consider it, either the option will seem unproductive and lose its charge, or you'll find it can spur you toward new action.

I take charge of taking the charge out of criticism.

Shine

Oने afternoon I took my father back to the neighborhood where he had grown up. We ate lunch at the White Tower Restaurant that he had watched being built in the 1930s: green-and-white ceramic tile floors and a stainless-steel lunch counter.

We sat on the squeaky stools and ordered burgers from an ancient waitress. Two places down, slouched over her stool, was a woman in her thirties, tattooed, wearing a blue leather vest and pants, bruises and needle marks on her arms; she was smoking. My father turned to her and gently reprimanded her, explaining that he himself had quit smoking cigarettes after forty years and if he could do it, he knew that she could, too.

Both the waitress and the young woman stared at him as if he were from another planet. My father smiled and ate his burger, oblivious to the woman's lifestyle or the waitress's shock. I felt the impulse to apologize to them for my father's behavior, but I also was touched by his concern for a younger person's health. In his innocent state, my father often shines light in the world by forgetting to be defended and proper.

Today I examine my own defenses and let go of one way I isolate myself from others.

Wind

Whether you're in the middle of a storm or enjoying a gentle breeze, parentcare is like the wind. The wind is always blowing even when it seems still. It can refresh or challenge you. Sometimes it turns suddenly. You'll have to make adjustments each time it shifts, and it might shift many times in a day. You can't fight it for very long: the common wisdom is to bend with it and follow the course it takes you. Also, like the wind, parentcare will animate some aspects of (your) nature and destroy others. And like the wind, you can see parentcare only through its effects on what and who it touches.

However the wind blows, I answer.

Enough Is Enough

When are you doing enough for your parents? Will you wait for them to tell you? Will you look to their doctors, your family, your friends; will you believe them? Perhaps you're waiting to no longer think to yourself: I should be doing more; I could be doing more; if only I could . . . then all would be well.

Enough is enough. It's like a koan but not as difficult to grasp. When you've done what you decided to do, it's enough. So when you wonder if you're doing enough, the real question is, enough for what purpose?

At the level of there being no more left to do, it's impossible because, as long as your parents are alive, there's always something else you can do for them. At the level of assuaging your guilt or seeking approval, no amount of doing ever frees you from such needs.

Practice trusting yourself: experiment a little, feel your way through caregiving. Don't allow yourself to be too easily swayed by your own doubts. You aren't a child anymore who can please your mom and dad by being good, helpful, or seen and not heard. You're finding your own balance. It's inside you. You won't recognize it through a thought or an emotion. It's an intuition, a knowing.

Today I do (did) enough.

Out of the Blue

"Your mother will be back in a little while. She went next door," my father said. But my mother has been dead for ten years. Out of the blue I was jettisoned back to when my mother was alive. Part of me wanted it to be true, and I suddenly felt her absence more deeply. This feeling made me angry, but I was able to breathe into the moment without explaining the facts of linear time to my father. I allowed him to be content in the moment.

When I am broadsided by a past, painful loss, I acknowledge that the past, revealed through my parent's timeless memory, may provide a window of opportunity for my own healing.

Talking Heads

Talking from your head is when you repeat what you are feeling or what you think you should be feeling without actually experiencing the emotions. It's confusing to others when you say you feel compassion but you act tense or aggravated. What you believe or read about parentcare and the experience you live through may not jibe. When you can slow down long enough to listen to your heart and not the information tape in your head, you may discover what support you need to be present to this day, to this moment.

Today I will let my heart inform me.

Sometimes It's No

*N*o is a powerful word. It's such a small word to make it easier to say. Imagine having to say *prestidigitation* every time you wanted to refuse something. Despite it being an easy word to pronounce for some of us, *no* is the hardest word to say, especially to our parents. Even when we do say it, we often feel so guilty or fearful of disapproval that we take it back.

There's an African proverb: if you are never angry, you are unborn. In a way, if you never say *no* your *yes* is unborn. Whenever we withhold or take back a *no*, we end up carrying resentments, blaming the other person and ourself. Then whatever we're doing is affected by our indignation.

There's a difference between not looking forward to doing something and feeling internally intruded on faced with doing it. What distinguishes one from the other is very individual. It isn't necessary to *justify* our personal distinctions to others. Sometimes it helps to explain our reasons, if a parent takes the step to ask.

No doesn't have to be loud or mean. But even when we say it gently, our parents may attempt to bully us, cajole us, or otherwise manipulate us into taking it back. Then we have to summon up the power to repeat it: *no*. It's a complete sentence in itself: when we say it to our parents *and* when they say it to us.

Today I accept no *into my life.*

Loyalty

One way to be loyal to parents is to uphold their beliefs. Gunner's parents believed in self-reliance. The children cleaned their own rooms and made their lunches for school each morning. When Gunner first began to care for his parents, he was loyal to their belief. He helped out only when one of them asked.

Gunner also stayed loyal to their teaching of self-reliance by trying to do all he could for them on his own. At first, he didn't consult any professionals or burden his friends with the details of his struggles or concerns. Within a year, it was clear his parents needed more help than they would ask for, and he had developed a low-grade flu that hung around for three months. Loyalty to his parents' values was interfering with caring for them and was making him sick.

Today I reexamine my loyalties and I reprioritize them if necessary.

Ageless and Timeless

There are times when we slip out of being an individual with a set personality relating to our particular parent and the history between us and experience ourself as the ageless, archetypal Daughter or Son attending to the essential Mother or Father. These moments strike each of us under different conditions, but uniformly they offer us a taste of timelessness. Madeleine Mysko relates such a moment in this poem:

Thursday

I have to kneel to wash my mother's feet.
Newly fragile from surgery,
She trembles in the shower, holds on tight
To the towel bar. She's balanced slippery
As infants I have lathered in this tub.
I send a silent prayer up through the steam:
"Don't let me let her fall." I hardly scrub,
But ceremoniously overcome
The awkwardness, and move the sopping cloth
Down my mother's legs, across her toes.
She thinks that she's a bother, but the truth
Is I am struck with piety and lose
Myself in washing her, like one ordained
To take another's precious feet in hand.

 When I care for my parent, we meet in timelessness.

Common Ground

What would you have if you eliminated the differences between you and your parents as they are right now: their physical state, their beliefs and attitudes? Pick any area. What's left is your common ground. It may be a very small spot or a vast expanse. In the daily morass of parentcare, returning to common ground—whether favorite foods, similar hairstyles, or a shared love of opera—is a way to reestablish your connection and equilibrium. When the shadier forces of old resentments and hurts plague your relationship, equilibrium allows you to give yourself some relief.

If resentment storms my consciousness today, I take shelter in the common ground I share with my parents. When the storm eases, I can reach my support system.

The Road to Nowhere

One of the greatest gifts of parentcare is being engaged in a process with no product in sight. You aren't caring for your parents to prevent them from dying. Of course you have goals: to help them be comfortable and safe and to experience a good death. But when they do die, you won't have a promotion, a medal, ultimate approval, a better marriage, stronger muscles, or lower cholesterol.

You give care out of some mixture of love and duty; in the process you also learn to do without outcomes. What freedom: not to be so mechanical, so return-oriented. You're acting for the sake of the action. You're letting go of the need to make sense of everything with your mind. You're developing trust. Perhaps in your uncertainty and anxiety you feel far away from that trust, but in truth, it's because you're giving up your attachment to control. Who said trust is a constant state of calm or peace of mind? It's a little like falling in love. The Danish philosopher Søren Kierkegaard said that anxiety is the dizziness of freedom.

Be patient. You're undoing years of living under the illusion of cause and effect. You're experiencing what Julia Cameron calls spiritual chiropractic—realigning your values and perceptions.

By letting go of control I'm experiencing the many aspects of freedom.

Praying for a Quick Death

As my father declined and the emotional burden was taking its toll on me, I prayed for his death. Sometimes my prayers were full of rage at God; other times I prayed like a martyr. At times I couldn't tell if I longed for his death so that my own suffering or his would end. But thoughts of his death and the relief it would bring consistently lingered at the edge of my consciousness for quite a while. Often it scared me. I was afraid that unconsciously I would be remiss in the quality of care I gave to him.

I felt incredibly guilty about believing that life would be easier for all concerned if he would just die. But it was true. I didn't know how I could trust myself feeling this way until I confided in a friend. She pointed out that by bringing this shadow side of myself out into the open, I was getting the help I needed to manage it. My friend reminded me, too, that I could honor my instincts without acting against my values.

So instead of berating myself for wishing for his death, I began a process inside: mentally picturing his absence and myself without a father. I was recognizing the difference between willing him to die and letting him go emotionally and spiritually.

There are safe ways to bring out my shadow side and discover the best way for me to honor its message.

007: The Refrigerator

Do you feel a little bit like a spy when you inspect your parent's refrigerator? Do you surreptitiously throw out what's spoiled, secretly take stock of the food supply, or slip food in when he's out of the room in hopes he will eat it? Maybe you don't want to embarrass your parent, maybe you are trying to avoid a confrontation, or maybe it makes you so sad that your parent needs help to eat well that you'd rather concentrate on being clandestine than on what you're doing and why. Whatever your reason, you have discovered a way to be playful with yourself, a way to relieve the heaviness of one of your caregiving chores. Go for it. Pick a code name for yourself. Hum the theme from a detective show. Lighten your burden with sport. Caregiving doesn't count more if it's no fun.

 I use playfulness wherever I can and let it lighten my spirit.

The Lucky Ones

B rent boasted that his eighty-one-year-old father beat him at tennis again and that his mother was healthy until the day the past year she died suddenly. I didn't know what to say. Had my family done something to deserve the protracted end stage of my parents' lives? Brent's family didn't have to confront the physical, emotional, and spiritual challenges we were facing every day. I no longer could imagine what my relationship with my parents would be like without the context of caregiving. I couldn't even imagine what I would be like in the world at large minus the experience. My family suffered a lot, and we learned a lot. We'd all faced aspects of love, spirit, bureaucracy, and pain that were as intense as they were new to us.

I was not King Arthur whose parents left him to take on the world on his own. I was more like the hero in the story of Iron John who had to return to his parents and steal the key from under their pillow as they slept, or Persephone who was ordained to keep returning to her mother.

Perhaps Brent's growth came through other experiences that life offered him. And perhaps my own family was one of the lucky ones, because, as hard as this time often was, the gifts were invaluable.

 *I am one of the lucky ones.*

Heart Protector

In the practice of acupuncture there is a pathway called the heart protector. The sense of protection includes both the idea of shielding or defending and the concept of cherishing. It is difficult to be an effective caregiver when you have abandoned your own heart. In such a state you're depleted. It takes greater effort to act. Momentary miracles such as an exchange between squirrels or an expression of appreciation from your mother are easily overlooked.

Take a nap, listen to a favorite song, leaf through a book of photographs, or go for a walk. If you feed your heart something every day, then even when it feels as though it's breaking, it still will be strong. It will protect *you.*

I champion and cherish myself by feeding my heart each day.

Brave and Uncertain

You and your parents are travelers, explorers. You're creating a path by walking it. You aren't following anybody else. There's a lot of uncertainty. It takes courage from all of you. Each of you is being brave in his or her own way. One of you is valiantly expressing himself, the other is fearlessly containing her anxiety; someone may be resolutely getting out of bed in the morning. Uncertainty is by turns frightening, exhilarating, and exhausting. Often creativity comes out of it. It's hard to gauge what takes courage for others to accomplish. You can't always recognize it, but if you try to now and then, you may get a glimpse of the bold clan with whom you travel.

I see the courage in myself and in my parents today.

Touch

Because of my role as a caregiver there were many instances when I was in physical contact with my father: helping him with his coat, combing his hair, assisting him with his seat belt. Inadvertently, we ended up touching a lot. My father never was much for physical affection with his children. Sometimes when I had to touch him he'd recoil as if my fingers burnt him. Other times I was the one who shuddered as if his wrinkled, veiny skin were dry ice. Then there were the moments when, unsolicited, my father would reach out and gently brush the lint off my shirt—even when there was none. Through a series of these interactions I began to notice that my father and I, perhaps unconsciously, were using touch to communicate with each other. His willingness to receive it and offer it was one way my father expressed the level of closeness he was feeling. From my end, how I felt about touching him became a gauge for the amount of emotional distance from or closeness to him I wanted to take care of myself.

Today I communicate with my parent and understand myself through my relationship to touch.

Left Out and Far Away

This may be your situation or someone in your family's:

You live far away from your parents. You may be able to make only one or two trips a year back home. You get reports on your parents' condition from other family members and health care professionals. Sometimes the reports conflict. You offer advice, but no one takes it. Your parents tell you they miss you. You feel guilty, frustrated, worried. You blame your siblings for your worry. They blame their stress on your absence.

On top of your concern for your parents, you're feeling a loss of your place in the family. Your love and concern have no avenue for expression. But they do! There may not be much hands-on care or decision making you can participate in. Could this be one of your life challenges—to find new ways to give? There's plenty you can do from far away. Give your parents the gift of connection to your far-flung life by sending them photographs and tape-recorded or written letters.

Through letters, e-mail, and the telephone you can support the caregivers: listen to them unload, affirm their decisions, and acknowledge their hard work. Even if they don't seem to appreciate it, continue to offer it. Don't be daunted by outcomes; give in your own way.

I don't let distance, my own or my siblings', get in the way of expressing love through caregiving.

The Art of Juggling

Dropping the ball is a normal part of juggling. If it weren't, juggling wouldn't be an amazing feat. Every time a juggler adds another trick or an extra ball, she falters dozens of times during practice. In the midst of juggling your own life with caring for your parents, you also will drop the ball on more than one occasion. If you didn't, parentcare wouldn't be such an amazing feat either.

My mistakes are the proof that I'm doing the best that I can performing a death-defying feat.

Shame

One day while waiting with my father in the dentist's office, he started to flirt with the receptionist. He wouldn't stop talking. He kept pacing up and down the waiting room; everyone was looking at him while I hid behind the newspaper.

Our parents' actions often make us feel ashamed of them—what they say in public, how they look, how they smell, how they move their bodies, the conditions they live in. We demand that they cool it, sit down, shut up, act normal. What will people think of us? Our reactions to them may embarrass our parents!

In our society we tend to hide untidy realities. We've been taught that aging is embarrassing and imperfect. Denying the natural order of life leaves us filled with shame. Our parents deserve our respect for living under such adversarial conditions.

Today I will hold up my head high when I am with my parent in public.

A Hard Day's Night

What you have to do today may not include the slightest kernel of joy. Maybe you're making arrangements to have a health care worker move into your parents' house, or you're going to the lawyer's office to discuss how to manage your parents' hard-earned money, or you must tell your father not to take his walks alone. To serve others often brings you to your own darkest moments. It is here that personal integrity and faith truly form.

Today I acknowledge the birth pangs of my courage.

After the Fall

In poet Madeleine Mysko's "Winter Green," a daughter describes her mother assimilating her new limitations after a third surgery. It's winter. Slabs of snow from the roof have slid off and broken a hedge. In the poem the hedge also symbolizes the mother. The daughter recognizes that her mother's life spirit hasn't been weakened by the limitations of aging and illness:

Winter Green

"Winter is no season for the frail."
This from my mother, aged seventy-three,
who, five days after her third surgery,
has left the cane behind her in the hall

and hobbled out in coat and hat to have
a look: a couple feet of snow, and now
slabs from the roof have crushed the hedge below.
Who knows how much of it's been broken off?

I look up from shoveling and watch
my mother watch her step. She's got respect
for ice, and for the gift of stepping out erect.
She'll go no further than the dripping porch.

Sudden reactions: a band of crows
shrieking across the road, a glint of sun
on icicle. And when I look again
I see it—precious and precarious—

that moment when she reaches out to break
the only chunk of ice her broom can reach.
I smell the green within the broken branch.
"This hedge," my mother says, "just might spring
   back."

🎁 *Today I celebrate the tenacity of my parent's life*
   spirit.

A Long, Cool Drink

A crucial element in parent caregiving often over-looked is to review your accomplishments and feel good about what you're doing: reaching the right person at the Medicare office, changing the lightbulb in your father's closet, sharing a joke with your mother. Seeing the good in what you are choosing to do creates more good. It makes you take your father's hand and decide to give it a little squeeze, and maybe you feel a squeeze back. Drink in the goodness you help to create in the world. Radiate your success; it isn't overblown pride. It's elixir.

Many people are afraid to embrace the good moments for fear that they'll have the rug pulled out from under them or that they'll spoil accomplishments by acknowledging them. These are hard beliefs to challenge in yourself. Try giving yourself permission for a few minutes each day to enjoy your successes and slowly increase your allotment over time. You may feel anxious at first, but stick with it and eventually you'll tap into a deep source of energy and well-being.

I drink in the goodness I help to create in the world.

Home

Oone morning as I got my father ready to go to the eldercare center, I noticed that the yard looked scraggly. After the van picked Dad up, I called on one of the neighborhood kids and hired her to mow the lawn. That afternoon I introduced my father to his new groundskeeper. He summarily ordered her out of the house and started to shout at me.

"Who do you think you are? It's my damn house and my damn lawn! Leave me alone!"

I was shocked and angry, but mostly I was embarrassed in front of the young girl. "The grass is uneven. It looks like an abandoned lot out there," I retorted.

"It's *my* lawn," he repeated as if I hadn't understood him the first time, "and it looks fine to me."

He was right. I was judging the lawn based on my standards that were once his standards, too. But he'd changed. It was more important for him to mow his own lawn than it was to make it even. My father had become enlightened. He had let go of the end result in favor of the process. Now it was my turn to do the same.

Today I suspend my judgment of standards in favor of the flow of experience.

Emotional Center

When you have brothers or sisters, often one of you becomes your parent's emotional center. This role may shift from one sibling to another over time, but if it's your turn, it's a demanding role in which to be cast. Your parent has selected you as her intimate other. At first you may feel fulfilled: you're her favorite, her confidante; you're special. Over time it also can feel like a huge weight: if you don't call or visit her enough she becomes angry and depressed. No matter how much time you spend with her it isn't enough, and she becomes jealous of your other close relationships. It can get uncomfortable if she complains to you about other relatives—she may even want you to intercede—and when she's upset, you bear the brunt.

On one hand you're the one she counts on, and you don't want to let her down. On the other hand, the situation is consuming your life. There's no easy solution. You set the limits you're able to set, enjoy the pleasurable moments of her confidence, and live with the guilt of not satisfying her needs and wishing you weren't her center. But you live: you take care of yourself first, because ultimately there's nothing worse for parents than to have sapped the life out of their offspring.

 *I'm my own emotional center before, during, and after I'm my parent's.*

Detachment

Many aspects of eldercare require detachment. Stepping back from your emotions about a situation often is necessary to act. Your feelings can be enormous enough to immobilize you when you take your parent for an MRI, or navigate through bureaucracies to secure care. It is OK to erect barriers against the overstimulation of difficult situations. This doesn't mean you're distant, less caring, unavailable, or without feelings. It means that out of a love for your parents and for yourself, you're keeping your emotions from sapping the energy you need to be effective; this is one of the highest forms of love. It's also often a welcome relief.

Visualize your emotions and your actions flowing in parallel streams. Notice them both and walk steadily between them.

*Today I practice detachment by moving calmly
between the stream of my emotions and my actions.*

Wit's End

Ellen's teenage daughter screamed at the top of her lungs: "I can't live with her anymore, she's making me crazy!" It had been a few months since Ellen's mother-in-law, Mary, had come to live with them. Knowing that she had to defuse the situation, Ellen, at her wit's end, took her daughter's hand and said, "Let's go for a walk." A few blocks into their walk, they passed a rally held for a group of teenagers who had walked across the country for world peace. Witnessing the commitment of her peers, Ellen's daughter turned to her: "I guess if these teens could walk three thousand miles for world peace, I can live with grandma."

Whether it's coincidence, fate, or faith, sometimes problems are resolved outside of my efforts.

All of the Work and None of the Credit

After Mrs. Klien, eighty-six years young, sold the family home, she moved to an apartment closer to her son. Because of Mrs. Klien's new proximity, her daughter-in-law, Carol, has taken over many of the regular caregiving tasks such as grocery shopping for Mrs. Klien. Mrs. Klien shares few of her emotions with Carol, saving them for her telephone calls and visits with her daughter, Ann. It makes Carol angry to do all the work without receiving the emotional rewards.

Carol is now the primary caregiver, but Ann is still her mother's primary emotional support. It's hard to do the chores if you're missing out on the feeling level of caregiving. This situation also can make you feel jealous and resentful of the person who is your parent's emotional support and of your parents. Tell them. It might not change their behavior, but it will transform you from being the silent sufferer.

It's time to refocus. Why are you participating in caregiving? What are you receiving that's valuable from the experience? Perhaps being the emotional center has its shortfalls (see page 150). Are you someone who gets caught up comparing yourself with others in your life?

There is growth for me in my circumstances right now.

Mind Games

When my father's dementia made it hard for him to remember who I was or the decade in which he lived, it didn't curtail his cleverness or the trickster aspect of his character. He hated to be told what to do. So, although he enjoyed the adult day care center, he devised ways of trying to get out of going. Left alone in the morning, he scribbled a sign and posted it on the front door: BUS, I'VE GOT A COLD. I'M NOT GOING TODAY. If one of us supervised his getting ready he had a series of tricks: eating very slowly; just when the van arrived, going to the bathroom and taking a long time grunting and groaning behind the closed door; and hiding his shoes, house keys, or all his underwear while he was dressing—anything to miss his ride.

My brother and I had different ways of responding to his tricks. I would tell Dad up front that he was going to day care even if I had to drive him myself. My brother, the firstborn, had his own tricks. He would let the bus leave without Dad and then invite him to go out for coffee. Afterward, they got back in the car and my brother dropped him off at the center.

Though it was often aggravating to get Dad going in the morning, it was also a joy to meet up with a part of him that remained intact despite dementia.

As the parent I once knew transforms, I unearth the ways he remains the self I recognize.

Links

I am linked to my parents, family, and friends through a network of relationships. Taking care of my parents has linked me to another set of relationships. If I drew a diagram, like a family tree, I could see the ways I have an interdependent link with many people. I also am linked to the future. My experiences with parent-care will influence others, even those who are unknown to me now. I'm playing a part in creating a future that includes positive caring for elders. My participation in forging values for the generations to come is my small but important part.

The way I walk in the world today is a ripple in the pond; it creates waves on the edges of the shore.

To Assume Makes an Ass *Out of* U *and* Me

Parentcare teaches you to give up assuming anything, especially if your parent has dementia. You never know what to expect of your parent's memory or perception of reality, often from moment to moment.

Like any new state of being, giving up your basic assumptions is scary. You're in brand-new territory. Anything can happen. Listen to yourself: are you already assuming "anything" means the worst things?

When you discover yourself either assuming the worst or assuming you know best about how to manage a situation, breathe deeply before you act: on the in-breath invite possibility into the picture, and on the out-breath let go of your assumptions. In time you'll find yourself becoming aware of more than you now imagine.

I let go of my assumptions and trust the outcome.

The Inscrutable Self

After being my father's primary caregiver for a while—shopping, preparing him for day care, housecleaning, doing yard work, acting as chauffeur and point person for the lawyer and the social work contacts—I felt as if I were my father's intimate partner, as if I knew everything about him. One afternoon while I was doing laundry, I came across a series of Polaroids in one of Dad's shirt pockets. They were photographs of him and a woman from the day care center dancing cheek to cheek, working on a quilt together, and eating lunch. He'd never even mentioned her to me.

A few weeks later I paid him an unexpected visit at the center. Dad was busy talking with a group of men. He waved at me. I approached and he introduced me as his son and went right on with his conversation. Standing in the parking lot, I felt a bit foolish. I mistook my position in my father's world. No matter how much he had come to depend on my help, he had his own life. I was not privy to every detail. Certain aspects of him would remain independent of me regardless of his physical or mental condition. I felt sad and relieved.

A bittersweet mystery is the separate unknowable aspects of each of us.

Giving

What more can you give? You give your time, your energy, your money—what more do they want? Probably one of the most basic spiritual principles is that giving and receiving are one in the same. When you view caregiving as giving away yourself, you can't recognize what your parents may be offering you.

If you can pause after preparing your mother's dinner and contemplate how this giving feeds you, you may open up to receiving a rich dessert.

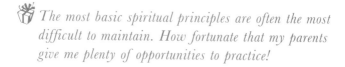 *The most basic spiritual principles are often the most difficult to maintain. How fortunate that my parents give me plenty of opportunities to practice!*

Details, Details

In the practice of Zen, attention to detail is one of the ways toward spiritual enlightenment—not the nit-picking type of attention but the kind that promotes awareness and focus. Look around your own home. What is the one simple action you can take that would improve the daily quality of your life? Why haven't you done it yet?

With regard to your parent, details might mean the difference between safety and an accident waiting to happen. Your parent's reason for letting certain details lapse can range from denial to being overwhelmed. If you take the lead in installing better lighting by the stairway or purchasing a telephone with an amplified receiver to improve hearing, safety and comfort will be restored. You might even feel motivated to do something comparable for yourself.

Remember, you don't have to take care of everything all at once. One simple change is a catalyst. It builds momentum for other details in their turn.

 Without stress I attend to one simple detail today that improves the quality of my own life or my parent's.

Thirty-Eight Messages

Returning from a weekend away, I arrived home to discover thirty-eight messages on my answering machine from my father, all of them identical. This was very painful, but I listened to every one to see if they would differ.

When we were young children, we liked to hear our favorite story read over and over. We moved our lips with the words, correcting the storyteller if she skipped over or changed a part. Knowing the story by heart felt soothing and safe. Knowing what came next made us feel in control.

When my parent repeats the same phrase or story, I can hear it as his personal mantra and I can be comforted by his ability to create a feeling of safety and control. Today I, too, will remember a story that soothes me.

Desire Reigns

In nature, spring is the time when most new life bursts into being. Even the old apple tree, gnarled and split, puts forth a few blossoms. But some flora bloom in fall or winter.

How natural it is that your parent may suddenly develop an infatuation with someone at the senior center or redecorate the night table with pictures of a high school sweetheart. Your parent's flirtation or crush is living proof that desire revitalizes us throughout a lifetime.

I look to my own feelings of desire to invigorate me.

Mental Health Day

To take care of anyone, you have to be able to take care of yourself. This is a simple statement that we all have heard before, but understanding it and doing it are two different things. It takes an amazing amount of energy to ride the waves of caring for elderly parents. You start out gung ho, but as the months roll by and then the years, it's hard to keep up with the pace you have set for yourself. A little time away—a day trip or a weekend on a regular basis—recharges the energy that's needed. Caring for parents also can be a time to learn how to care for yourself. Only a Higher Power has a limitless source of energy. Plan and take a mental health day.

Today I take time for myself. By accepting my limits, I open up to a limitless spiritual power of faith.

Eccentricities

At one point my father began collecting one-liter plastic soda bottles which he filled with tap water. The kitchen counter was covered, the refrigerator full. They began to line the windowsills. I would empty them out and throw them away only to find them reappear overnight. It was driving me crazy.

One day my father said to me, "I don't know why you're collecting those bottles of water, but to each his own."

If my parent needs to ritualize an activity that is harmless, I can give up my desire to maintain the status quo and join in.

A Thread in the Fabric

When I talk to people who haven't experienced caring for their parents yet, they often seem grateful the topic has come up. Of course, there are those who are indifferent, but most people are interested and many discuss their own parents, speculating about the future, sometimes for the first time. One man I sat beside on a plane said, "I guess my sister will take care of Mother." Then he had a quizzical look and mused, "But if things change, I may have to do it."

Not only had I learned through being a caregiver, but I was a conduit through which others would start to consider their future and parentcare. Often at a party, in the gym, or in transit, if the conversation turns to parentcare, the person with whom I'm speaking will utter a quick, ironic laugh and say just what I once said: "I suppose I never realized that after I left home my parents would become such a big part of my life again."

🎁 *The value of my experiences with parentcare reach beyond me and my family.*

Crying

Rain

Each storm-soaked flower has a beautiful eye.
And this is the voice of the stone-cold sky:
"Only boys keep their cheeks dry.
Only boys are afraid to cry.
Men thank God for tears
Alone with the memory of their dead,
Alone with lost years."

Vachel Lindsay

In Vachel Lindsay's poem, he reminds us that as the beauty of a flower grows out of the rain that soaks it, so the tears we humans cry keep us company and soak our soul in what makes us beautiful. There are many reasons to cry while we're involved in parentcare: when a parent is in pain, when a parent hurts our feelings, when we're frustrated, and when we're moved by an intimate moment. Crying is a release that physically and emotionally relieves our pent-up pain. It's more than OK to cry. It's good for you.

 Today I let tears flow, whether it's a single drop or a heavy rain, and my body and soul are made supple.

Unbelievable

Your mother has just had a successful lung cancer operation and the first thing she does at home is light up a cigarette. How can she blithely continue doing exactly what gave her a life-threatening illness in the first place? It's, well, unbelievable. You want to shake some sense into her or throw up your hands and give up on caring for her if she won't care for herself. There are other options.

Look at your own life. Isn't there something unbelievable you've done: not the foolish or self-destructive things you regretted later, but the illogical, downright obviously-against-the-current-of-sense thing? If you've never done anything like that, be prepared; you will.

As elders, our parents have a different perspective on their lives than we do. No longer needing to support a family, and having the long view of life, death, and suffering, our parents are in a better position to decide what they're willing to risk for the sake of pleasure from life and in relating to death on their terms.

So when your father orders three eggs and a side of bacon after his bypass operation, take a deep breath; yes, he's being selfish, but that's not why he's doing it. It's because he has entered the realm of the unbelievable. Wish him well out there.

 *I recognize the many realms of living and wish my parents well in theirs.*

Surprise

Half the days when my father went to the adult day care center, he would complain about having to go. I knew from the staff reports and his general sense of well-being that he actually enjoyed going there; he just didn't like to feel he was being sent somewhere. So when he grumbled on the mornings I came by to help him dress and be sure he got in the pickup van, I endured his griping and said nothing. Then came the day when the combined pressures of my life got the better of me. That morning when he began his harangue, I added my own lament. I told him I was angry about showing up every morning to help him and hearing nothing but complaints. For a moment he was quiet. He sat down and said he'd had no idea I was upset. He apologized to me. He went on to tell me that he was full of anger over having dementia and that he had needed some way to blow off steam. He thanked me for helping him.

Nothing much changed after that. He continued to gripe and I don't think he ever acknowledged his dementia or thanked me for helping him again, but in that moment my father and I had the relationship I'd hoped for as an adult.

Sometimes when I'm open with my parents, I create an opportunity for them to connect with me.

Perfect Mistakes:
Some Notes on Failure

1. Parentcare is not a test.

2. The right thing to do is whatever works.

3. If what I'm doing isn't working, I take Samuel Beckett's advice: try again, fail again, fail better.

4. Human beings weren't constructed to be perfect.

5. Success is inevitably built on a series of failures.

6. Trying harder doesn't always lead to doing better.

7. If the end of the story isn't written, how do I know I've failed?

8. Only those who live in a world of strict duality and opposites believe in success and failure.

9. I never fail as long as I've learned.

Today I choose one "note" and I say it aloud to myself in front of a mirror fifty times.

Creativity

At the adult day care center, my father attended an art class. He brought home the objects he made and displayed them on a bookshelf like trophies. I winced at first. They reminded me of the displays of our childhood—clay ashtrays and handprints. Then he began painting: strong, bold, and decisive images. One of his paintings was incorporated into the design for the day care center's new garden gate. All my life my father had insisted he wasn't the creative type, despite having two children who are visual artists.

With the help of dementia, my father had finally shed his beliefs and conditioning and touched his own spirit. I no longer was embarrassed by his works of art. I was overjoyed. When the oldest apple tree blossoms, the flowers are especially delicate and beautiful set against the scarred and wizened trunk.

Today I find a way to touch the creative spirit in my parents and in myself.

Separating Spouses

When one of your parents must live in a nursing home while the other remains in an independent living situation, a line has been crossed that's profound. However long your parents have lived their life in tandem, they never will sleep together again, never cuddle up on the couch, or experience the sense of well-being from hearing one another from separate parts of the house. Each of them may suffer anxiety, depression, anger, and grief, even if the independent parent has a sense of relief from the burden of caregiving.

Your relationship with both of them will change, too. Once you related to them as a unit, and now you can't count on the ways that they balanced each other. They may become more exaggerated versions of themselves, or they may exhibit traits you've never encountered in them. My father, who was always an unflappable character, became anxious when he was separated from my mother for she was the one that expressed distress. You may be interacting with your parents as individuals for the first time in your adult life. Like all change, it will be difficult, but like all change, it will reveal a great deal to you.

 Today I take nothing in my life for granted, for all things change.

A Swarm of Bees

Feeling overwhelmed by all you have to do can immobilize you. It's like your brain is invaded by a swarm of bees and the rest of you is drained of energy trying to fight them. You've got to get the buzzing out of your head.

Some people make a to-do list on paper and prioritize each item. Others arrange objects on their desk to represent each task—bigger objects for bigger problems. I use a sheet of paper, make headings for all the areas of my life, and write down what must be accomplished under each. A friend of mine expels the swarm by talking about everything she needs to do in a marathon telephone session with a friend.

You can accomplish things only one day at a time. If you trust that you're not given more than you can handle at once, you can work through your list with confidence rather than out of stinging fear and anxiety.

Today is the tomorrow I worried about yesterday.

Holidays

As his dementia progressed, my father didn't seem to remember or care about the holidays. Involving him in social situations included a lot of extra work and anxiety. Someone had to help him shower, shave, and dress, and then someone had to take care of him during the celebration. There was also no telling if he would enjoy himself or enter a spell of anger or grief. As a family, we were torn between wanting our father to participate and wanting the holiday to be pleasant.

One Thanksgiving, it was my turn to bring my father to dinner. As he showered and I picked out his clothes, all the Thanksgivings past came back to me; I opened to the season. I dressed him with the reverence of the page to an aged monarch. He gazed in the mirror, nodding with approval. I had no idea if the dinner would go smoothly, but I knew that for the moment we were both truly thankful. We walked to the car beaming, father and son, dressed up in thanksgiving.

Holiday means holy day. Holidays stir up deep emotions, and it is hard to include an aging parent who could wreak havoc on the day. But holidays are more than festivities; they are a demarcation of time, a ritual that pulls people together as another year progresses, a day when holy things take place.

 In person or in spirit I bring my parent's presence to holy days.

Agony

Parentcare is a stage of life in which the chances are that you'll witness agony. Agony is an aspect of all our lives that we dread and avoid whenever we can.

The word itself is derived from the Greek, *agon*, meaning a contest. Agony is a contest between us and another force. We talk about *fighting* the pain and *overcoming* despair. We're engaged in a competition, often a battle. It takes all our strength, determination, and endurance. A force is attempting to outdo us and we're trying to hold our ground and regain the upper hand.

When a parent is in a state of agony, she's using all her energy to match her opponent. If it's physical, it can be agony for you to witness her struggle, especially if she's defeated. You want to stop it. You suffer, too.

There's a saying that whatever doesn't kill you makes you stronger. In the case of agony, even if it does take your parent's life, she has become a hero in the process. This isn't a romantic vision of suffering, and nobody hopes a loved one will experience pain. Rather, agony causes a person to reach her limits, to stare the worst in the face; an aspect of the sublime.

Agony needn't be prolonged unnecessarily or rejoiced over, but when it can't be refused a contest begins, a transformation commences, and grace waits patiently.

 Today I honor the metamorphosis my parent undergoes dueling with agony.

Go Outside

Do you spend time with your parents doing nothing? So much of caring for them involves goal-oriented activities: shopping, doctors' appointments, decision making.

When care becomes all chore and no meditation, and your mind is fixated on getting things accomplished, go for a walk with your folks. Be sure that none of you has a destination in mind. Often you get further by having nowhere to go. It gives the body, mind, and spirit a chance to realign.

Walking outside helps the process. As all of you move together and breathe in the fresh air, you reestablish your connection beyond the surface of who's caring for whom. The bigger picture reemerges. You return to the rhythm of being together. Even if your parent is in a wheelchair or confined to bed, go outside together. Find a way to move in time, in step, without the confines of walls.

Today I let the outside into me and my parents.

Gone but Not Forgotten

Carlotta, an only child, had been visiting her mother weekly in a nursing home for more than a year. She was shocked and deeply hurt the first time her mother didn't recognize her. The two women had been visiting and talking for a half hour when Carlotta's mother started talking about her daughter in the third person. In a way Carlotta felt as if she had disappeared. She was devastated.

By the third time her mother didn't recognize her, Carlotta was prepared to explore this new circumstance. Rather than reminding her mother who she was, Carlotta encouraged her mother to speak about her daughter. Carlotta was by turns moved and intrigued by how her mother portrayed her. It was a unique position to be in, to be the proverbial fly on the wall as her mother talked.

Over the next year, there were some days her mother recognized her and some days when she didn't. Either way, Carlotta found the time with her mother precious and rewarding.

In each new circumstance is an opportunity.

One Death

The death of one of your parents propels you into one of the most challenging situations of parent-care: caring for your surviving parent who is in a state of grief while you experience your own mourning. If you're fortunate, you and your parent can console each other and slowly lead one another into a new version of your life. But often the difference between losing a parent and a spouse can't be bridged by your shared love.

One common image of mourning is to spend a period of time in darkness and then reemerge into the light of the living. It can happen in stages or through ritual all at once. The time and energy it requires varies from one person to another. Your parent may or may not be able to complete the journey, but you must. In this way you may have to let go emotionally of your living parent as well as the one who died. You cannot wait like a young child for your parent to meet you in the light.

I complete my mourning journey with or without my surviving parent.

Remember Now

Do you ever take stock of your achievements? It helps you to clarify what you want to do next and to feel capable and worthwhile. Some people look back on their lives annually as a way of putting them in perspective. Others review their journeys every five or so years.

If you wait until their funerals to review your parents' lives, you deprive them and yourself of many of the benefits. Whatever combination of photographs, films, memorabilia, and stories are available, create a time to honor your parents' lives in review. It will expand your perspectives, it will give your parents a way of communicating how they want to be remembered, and if you have children, it helps them to see themselves on the journey, too.

Acknowledging the value of my parents' life journeys helps me and my children explore our own places in the world.

The Handwriting on the Wall

B esides leaving little notes around the house to remind himself of things, my father would leave notes for me:

Geo, I picked thirty-two strawberries and six tomatoes today.—Love, Dad.

To the Boss, *Reader's Digest* called. I may win.—Your Dad.

As his dementia progressed, his handwriting became shaky. There were breaks in his script, misspellings, and left-out words. I always had been struck by the resemblance of our handwriting. Now those likenesses were erased. My own writing was the vestige of his hand. His notes became a map of the changes taking place within him—a trail from his mind. I started collecting them.

Those notes, sad or funny, were some of the small but important intimacies between my father and me. It was a way he reached out to me. Getting a note, even a cantankerous one, could uplift my whole day. As dementia made the content of his notes hard to understand, I stayed connected to the intimacy of them by recognizing the growing distance from which my father had to struggle to reach me.

Today I decipher the emotional messages in my parent's writings.

Moving In

The decision to live with your parents changes your life. It's an arrangement that often lasts for years. It's a very personal decision and at the same time it affects everyone else in your life, even if you live alone. If you are doing it or considering it, it's because powerful forces are moving within you. It's crucial that you identify these forces, listen closely to them, and clearly hear their petition. You may want to go through this process with the aid of a counselor.

We know people for whom the decision to live under the same roof with a parent has been a blessing even with the enormous difficulties. These people weren't seeking approval or doing it out of obligation or guilt.

If you need permission not to live with your parents, with all our empathy, respect, and heartfelt trust, we give that permission to you here and now. If you decide to live with your parents, be prepared to revisit the wounds of your childhood in waves and torrents and fortify your support system; you've chosen an honorable and feral path.

I love and care for my parents in my own way, which is the right way for all of us.

Crabs

Your parent may not be a lovable, venerable, gray-haired sage. He might be disenchanted, bitter, insulting, and just plain crabby. Constantly hearing him talk about how terrible life is now compared to the past, or how fruitless life is, isn't good for you. No amount of understanding of the history or psychology behind your parent's crabbiness obliges you to have to listen to hours of negativity. Maybe other people can listen to him complain—friends, a counselor—and not become emotionally drained. But even if no such person exists, you have the right to protect yourself from his negativity. If pointing out the effects that his complaining has on you doesn't curtail it, you may have to limit the length of your visits.

I protect myself from overdosing on negativity.

The Life of the Party

Anniversaries and birthdays don't stop being important just because your folks are aging. As much as they say they don't care and it's too much trouble, it may be more important for them and you than you realize. Of course, numerous anxieties are associated with making a gathering: you could become flooded with memories that sadden you, your parents could act uninterested or ungrateful, or they could be too sick or too tired to stay for the cake. Tension might arise among siblings, family, and friends over a myriad of issues, including the awareness that this could be the last celebration that includes your parents.

With all these minuses, what are the pluses? Honoring elders also honors your own endurance and the value of family in all its forms. By acknowledging a birthday or anniversary, you affirm more than the individuals. Remember, you don't have to plan an extravaganza. Quiet and simple celebrations are equally significant. And even if you live far from your parents or you aren't on good terms, you can still commemorate their special day with a gift, a letter, a card, a prayer.

In person or in spirit, I celebrate my parents' significant occasions with them, and in the process I enrich myself.

Holiness

One afternoon when I went to pick up my father at the day care center, I observed John, a former doctor who now had Alzheimer's, in the center's garden with his wife. She was tenderly and patiently leading him to a bench. He shuffled slowly and hesitantly. As they sat down together and held hands, their love was apparent in the way they both leaned against each other. What seemed important in the flurry of my busy life receded in the presence of this intimate and holy moment.

Today I set aside my self-importance to notice and to experience a holy moment in the midst of decline.

Driven over the Edge

Your mother repeats the same panic-driven words: "I can't find my wallet!" Totally obsessed, she proceeds to tear apart the house. By now, you've learned to lead her into another train of thought, but it doesn't always work. Then you find yourself caught up in the frantic energy of the search, only to find the wallet in her pants pocket or in the refrigerator. Her anxiety is temporarily relieved, but you are left holding it.

I can't always separate myself from my parent's obsessions and anxieties. I am human and influenced by many forces outside of myself. I will take a deep breath now and let go of her anxiety.

Tricks of Fate

Fate plays marvelous tricks sometimes. Will's mother, Elizabeth, is eighty years old and a piano player in the style of Stephen Foster. Will schooled himself in rock-and-roll guitar. To him, his mother's music sounded rigid. She could play only the score in front of her. All during Will's adult life, when they tried to play together, he would become bored and frustrated with her stiff renditions. Similarly, Elizabeth found her son's free-form style sloppy and unmusical. It was a disappointment for both of them that they couldn't meet in the realm of a mutual passion.

As Elizabeth's dementia accelerated, she lost her inhibitions along with some of her capacities of concentration. When she played a piece of music, she could read only the skeleton of its structure. Unable to hold on to the notes, her fingers went with the rhythm. Because of the dementia, Elizabeth and Will finally could jam together. Mother and son were delighted.

Today Elizabeth can't play the piano anymore, but Will's relationship with her and his music was deepened by their breakthrough duets.

With the loss of old abilities, sometimes new opportunities present themselves.

I stay aware of and partake in whatever new opportunities present themselves as my parent's former abilities fall away.

Too Many Chefs

D ad says, "I don't want any strangers in my house."
One brother declares, "A full-time aide is over-reacting."

"Hey, Mom and Dad are doing fine on their own," says the other brother.

"I'll do whatever everyone decides," Mom offers.

"Who's going to pay for this?" pipes in your spouse. You say, "Help!"

Being from the same family doesn't guarantee that you'll have a single perspective on a situation or hold similar values. In fact, it may guarantee that you won't! Even if it's only you and one parent, there are just as many voices inside your head screaming to be heard.

There is no right answer. For many people, writing down a list of pros and cons for each option is a useful step when determining what to do. These lists are most valuable when you assign a degree of importance between one and ten to each item, one representing the most minor factor and ten representing the major one.

Whether you're negotiating with family members or the various voices in your head, a decision emerges, often haltingly, and leaves you less with a sense of relief and more with a sense of tentative optimism.

 *Today I listen to the quietest voices as I consider decisions.*

Can't *and* Should

Adhamola calls and invites you to meet him at a coffee bar. You say you *can't*, you've got too many calls to return. Charlotte invites you to go to a play; she's got the tickets. You decline, saying you *should* do some Medicare paperwork for your parents. It's true that some people have to slow the pace of their social life to make room for parentcare, but if socializing comes to a screeching halt, you'll be the one in need of care.

Feeling overwhelmed, deenergized, or depressed is increased by *can'ts* and *shoulds*. They immobilize you. Although at first you may not feel it, they're a sign of depression. In the midst of such a state, it takes sheer power of will to say *I can* as despair is pulling you into its depths. Even if you don't feel like it, do one thing for the sake of joy as a spiritual practice. For example, take time to watch the sunset with your child. The joy is not a detour; it doesn't take you off the road you *should* take. It's a shortcut, the reward for your courage as a traveler.

 Today I can accept taking time to enjoy without shoulding *on myself.*

The Director

Y ou may be sitting in the director's chair, but your parents are behind the doors with the gold stars on them, and we all know how temperamental stars can be. The director demands a scene be played a certain way and the star walks off the set. The director refuses to give in and the production is temporarily halted. Needing to be right and focusing on winning can cause more conflict than resolution. Why is it important for you to be right? For most problems there's usually more than one good solution. Losing feels like all your work has been wasted when you're more focused on issues of power than on resolving a dilemma. Just as the best directors listen to their actors, strong caregivers listen to their parents. When you give up on winning, you win.

In all my relationships I practice the difference between caring and winning.

The Coast Is Never Clear

It had been about two years since I had taken my father's car away, so I was taken aback when he had a tirade as if it had happened yesterday. He was just as angry and abusive. First I tried to explain to him that he hadn't had the car for two years. It was useless. He accused me of trying to convince him that he was crazy. I took a few deep breaths and spoke the same words I had two years earlier. Except this time I felt no anxiety. He railed about a week before letting go. I used my support system for reassurance that his fit would pass. I saw how far I'd come at integrating parentcare into my life and another way it had changed me for the better.

Even if I don't see them, transformations are taking place within me because of my caregiving role.

Overdoing It

Doesn't it feel good to push yourself sometimes? When you swim a few extra laps, stay up late into the night finishing a novel, put up one more shelf in the study, or weed the last row in the vegetable garden, it can be exhilarating. A continual diet of overdoing is harmful, but now and then it beefs up your sense of vitality. The same is true for your parents. Shoveling the walk could well be a strain on her heart. Standing on a rickety step stool to change a lightbulb can be dangerous. But if your parents are overextending themselves, even when help is available, they might need to overdo for the health of their spirit. Don't stop them. You can't monitor their lives anyway. They're following their instincts, living according to their definition of life. Grab a shovel and offer to pitch in, or ask if you can steady the stepladder. If they refuse your help completely, stand back, admire their gumption, and have a refreshing drink ready for them when they're done.

🎁 *Today I live and let live as a way of caregiving.*

Pain

I returned home after a weekend away to the news that my father was hospitalized. The diagnosis was pneumonia. Just a few days before I'd had difficulty getting him up and ready for day care. He insisted he was just a bit tired. The staff at the day care center didn't notice anything unusual about him.

When the doctor placed her stethoscope on his chest, my father touched his side and winced. The doctor asked him if his side hurt. "No," he replied. The same thing happened several more times. Each time my father denied he was in pain. Was this his way of coping with it and putting on a good face? Was dementia causing him to forget the pain before he could report it? How many times had I been unaware of his pain because he couldn't tell me? There was no way to know.

Once when I was young, he broke his shoulder and waited two days until the weekend to go to the hospital so that he wouldn't lose his wages. This man had been protecting all of us from his pain throughout his life. Either the dementia now was protecting him from suffering, or his own will was more powerful than the condition that infiltrated his body.

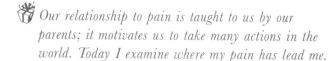 *Our relationship to pain is taught to us by our parents; it motivates us to take many actions in the world. Today I examine where my pain has lead me.*

Coping

Carpenters use a tool called a coping saw to cut detailed finish work. It's a special saw with thin, little blades that excel in cutting curves and intricate shapes. In parentcare, you also need special coping tools to maneuver through the daily morass of issues you confront. You probably have coping methods that have served you well over the years, but parentcare is a new stage. The carpenter can't use the same saw she used to cut wood to attend to the fine details. In the same way, you can't always rely on your former coping strategies to manage the fine details of carving out your own life while caring for your parents.

Once you have a coping saw or strategy, the trick to using it is to understand the wood you're cutting. Each variety has a different texture and is either hard, medium, or soft. You can't work redwood the same way you work a hard hickory. In the same way you have to modify or adjust your coping strategy to fit a variety of situations that are particular to parentcare. You need a coping saw and you need to learn all the ways to use it.

 Today I pick a new coping strategy and practice using it.

Excuse Me

In the sunroom of the nursing home, on a beautiful April day, Ella Lou's mother, a terminally ill cancer patient, politely interrupted the discussion, "Excuse me everyone. I have to throw up." Her dignified manner during a normally undignified moment marked a change that set the incident in Ella Lou's memory. Her mother had taught her to hold her feelings in and not to show the world that anything was wrong. Now her mother was in a compromising position and found a way to handle it in keeping with her values. At the same time, she passed on to her grown daughter a new method to deal with difficult feelings that come up at inopportune moments: graciously but forthrightly.

We may view our parents as unchangeable because in one way or another they've been an anchor for us. During the last phase of their life, often they are more flexible than we are.

I recognize the value of growth through the last moment of a day, a relationship, a life.

Big Mind, Small Mind

We have a big mind and a small mind. The big mind is part of our collective consciousness; it's what makes us feel connected to one another, nature, and spirit. The small mind is ego-based, limited, and defensive. Because of its size, the small mind wants to puff up and take over. It has something to prove. But the small mind isn't all negative. We need it also.

Parentcare is a practice that teaches you how to become fluid, moving from small mind to big mind. When your mother blows up at you, when all you've done is schedule a doctor's appointment for her, your small mind wants to argue: you *aren't* trying to run her life! Your big mind understands that your mother's accusations are based on her emotional reality. So with your big mind you negotiate a peace within yourself to negotiate peace with her; you don't argue or defend yourself. You speak from your heart and with respect.

When I had to leave work early to make arrangements for my parents, my partner accused me of overburdening him. I had to consciously move out of my small mind. It wanted to fight fire with fire by bringing up the times that I covered for him. I had to reach into my big mind to recognize that my partner was a member of my life who was affected by parentcare.

I practice moving from small mind to big mind.

Action Hero

Take a moment to look back at all the actions you've taken in the past month related to parentcare. Include the telephone calls, the conversations, the reading and writing, the thinking, and the decision making, along with activities such as grocery shopping and unstopping the toilet. You're an action hero: Superman or Wonder Woman. Action heroes aren't perfect, they're caring.

Feel the thrill of accomplishment in winning your inner and outer struggles. It takes as much courage, resilience, and strength to take action after action on behalf of your parents as it does to keep all of Gotham City from harm.

Unless you acknowledge and celebrate your successes, they lose their power to nourish you. When no one is looking, tie a sheet, towel, or tablecloth over your shoulders like a cape and run far and fast enough to feel it rise from your body. Ridiculous? Try it.

Today at least once, and then as many times as I feel like it, I utter the action hero cheer for myself: SHAZZAM!

By Hook or by Crook

Alex's plane arrived late. He rushed to the hospice to see his father. The doors were locked, and the nurse inside motioned him away, pointing to the visiting-hours sign. Undaunted and driven by an inexplicable urge, he walked around the building, checking doors and peering into windows. He spotted his father whose sliding-glass window was open. Quietly entering the room, Alex sat beside the sleeping man he always saw as inaccessible. Feeling a great peace, Alex fell asleep. He spent the next three weeks at his dying father's bedside, but it was that first night that he broke through a way of feeling.

When an urge to connect with your parents arises, trust it beyond the closed doors of propriety. No one can tell when a sacred moment will arrive. The heart doesn't work on a time clock.

Today I open the closed doors of propriety and let a sacred moment arrive.

Coming Home

When her mother was ill, Lynn commuted between Baltimore and Pennsylvania until her mother's death. When her father was diagnosed as having terminal cancer, he went to live with Lynn. Stan was a man of his times; he didn't display emotions about his condition. He talked about the removal of pieces of his body like they were car parts. Lynn had to give up her hope of having heartfelt talks with him. The only time Stan let his feelings surface was when he spoke about leaving his daughter alone in the world. And he would not mention it in her presence.

When she accepted his limits, she was able to appreciate other ways they'd become closer. Lynn acknowledged there was a door she never could open in her father, but she did open the door to her home.

 Today I look to the door I can open.

Waiting for the Word

In the legend, King Dionysus invites Damocles to an extravagant banquet. When he arrives, Damocles is seated beneath a sword suspended above his head by a single thread. So concerned over the precariousness of the sword, Damocles is unable to partake of the sumptuous feast before him.

The sword of Damocles is probably the image that best captures the period of waiting for your parent's diagnosis. With every medical test or doctor's visit, the sword sways a little. When will it fall? The anxiety is disarming. Ironically, feeling powerless to act can spur you into feeling an almost godlike power. You may find yourself making bargains with God yourself: if only my mother is OK I promise to. . . . Maybe you try to focus your entire will on making your parent well.

The hardest part of waiting for a diagnosis is accepting that it isn't what makes your parent healthy or ill. She's already in the state that the test results report. You don't let your parent down when, rather than concentrating on, or attempting to negotiate with, the upcoming diagnosis, you fill yourself up with a good novel, a few hours of shopping, or a visit to a friend. Giving to yourself is more fruitful preparation than sapping your energy with worry, especially if the prognosis is illness.

🎁 *I prepare myself with self-care instead of worry.*

Singing the Blues

I'm so down and out,
don't know what to do,
I've cried a thousand tears
and Dad still gives me these blues!

There are many reasons the blues evolved. One is that the soul needs to wail. Feeling deeply sorry for your own pain is normal. Neglecting to express it keeps the pain festering.

Enter the blues: put on your favorite tune, crank up your stereo, pick up your hairbrush or carrot microphone, lock the door, and wail. There is *nothing* better when you've got those doggone, elderly-parents-need-more-than-I-can-give blues.

Whether I think I can sing or not, I add my voice to the songs that release and nurture me.

The Will to Live

My father insisted that he wanted no extraordinary means to keep him alive, but the first time he was in the position of having to make the choice, he opted for the extraordinary. By the second time he was faced with the decision, he'd changed his mind again.

The whole family was in conflict. We tried to second-guess him: was he in a temporary depression, was he afraid of the pain, was he really ready to die if he couldn't sustain life on his own steam? We felt confused because his attitude had changed, twice.

We were looking at his decision as if it were any other—you decide and that's that. Maybe you change your mind, once. But the decision whether to use extraordinary means to sustain your own life isn't the same as choosing a vacation spot or buying a car.

Our father's relationship to his death was evolving. None of us could predict the shifts nor monitor them, not even Dad, because he was in the thick of the process. Finally, we had to let go and trust him to trust himself. After all of our caregiving, it was difficult not to intervene. It was also our final gift to him: a complete return of his life to him to do with as he saw fit.

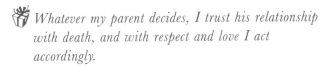

Whatever my parent decides, I trust his relationship with death, and with respect and love I act accordingly.

Cocoon

By middle age we recognize that life is in constant process and we begin to understand the spiritual meaning of transformation. Our aging parents are in the process of transforming. Their bodies, no longer so resilient to the forces of time and gravity, have begun to give way. Occasionally, our parents appear somewhat translucent and we recognize a spirit within them more alive than their bodies. The body is a cocoon for the soul. As hard as it is for us to let go of all that binds us to the earth, including the physical body, it is awesome to recognize the butterfly within it.

Today when I observe the lines of age and signs of weakness in my parents' bodies, I take a second look to penetrate the outer husks and recognize the souls.

Cradling

One evening during my mother's illness, I sat beside her on the couch with my arm around her. She was very tired. She leaned against me and tucked her legs up under her. I listened as she spoke, then cried, then dozed. I gathered her up to carry her to her bedroom. For a moment, I just sat and held her cradled in my arms that way. She had become smaller and more frail, but instead of feeling I was soothing her—the way I felt cradling a child—I felt completely encompassed by her as if I were the one nestled. In that instant the essence of her mothering held both of us and we were comforted. I rocked us until she fell asleep.

Today I open to receive what I give.

The Incredible Shrinking World

Many elders become isolated because of the demands of a world with which they no longer can keep pace. This separation doesn't always mean that something is wrong with them. How long we maintain interest in worldly things varies. Some ninety-year-olds are deeply connected to the outer world, but many aren't. The more important question is, as your parents' outer world shrinks, is their inner world expanding?

Your parents have accumulated a wealth of experience from which to draw and contemplate. They probably enjoy activities that stimulate them to do so: books, lectures, films, conversation, writing, painting, looking at art, and listening to music are just some of the activities that grace a rich inner life.

So what if your parents were never intellectuals, never readers; they still have souls. Anyway, your parents aren't as they were. They're metamorphosing. Ravaged and slumped in a chair in front of a television in the nursing home is not their inevitable fate.

You can't make your parents draw from their inner world, but you can support them in doing so. Listen to music together and discuss it. Read your dad a favorite poem. Don't abandon their inner lives by focusing solely on caring for their outer world.

Today I visit my parents' inner lives.

Metaphors

A fascinating part of being a person is recognizing the metaphors that appear in our otherwise ordinary lives. Particularly when we are feeling stress or are involved in a crisis experience, metaphors abound.

While on a walk, you notice a tree that recently has been hit by lightning. Though the branches scattered thirty feet from the tree are damaged, they still live; you connect it to your father's heart attack.

The lock breaks on your door and it symbolizes the way you feel locked out of your family because of decisions they've made over your objections.

The indirect light from your kitchen window creates a glow in the room. It reminds you of Rembrandt's painting *The Return of the Prodigal Son* and you relate it to your return to your parents' lives. Metaphors also can harbor premonitions or insights into our lives.

I am alert to the way metaphors are a source of revelations concerning parentcare.

Masterpiece

Creating a masterpiece is full of challenges, struggles, and joys. Every brushstroke of a painting documents a passage of time and a color to match the experience. Many dabs create images; the images create a story. The story is complex and rich. This is also true of the life journey of your parents. Because you are so close to the parent painting, you can't see the composition, or achieve a fresh perspective on it. You have to stand back from the canvas. Don't step back to make judgments concerning their choices but to appreciate the work involved. It has taken a lifetime for them to accomplish; it's taken a great effort.

🎁 *My parents are masterpieces.*

Have a Good Death

We all die. It's inevitable. If we're lucky, we can prepare for it. Be lucky. Help your parents be lucky. As a caregiver, you have the ability to assist your parents and yourself to have a good death. Realistically, this is the most any of us can expect.

To have a good death means to have a sense of completion. Write down a plan of action. It might include your parent's wishes with regard to extraordinary means of life support, funeral arrangements, burial wishes, and distribution of legacies. It also might include a list of people your parent wants you to inform in person, and items to include in the obituary. It can be as detailed as your parent wants to make it. I know a man who wrote his own eulogy that his daughter read at the funeral service.

It isn't morbid to consider these death questions or to approach your parents with them. The details of death and dying are best known to all family members so there isn't a lot of confusion and tension to add to everyone's grief.

A good death is one of the greatest gifts you can give someone. For your parents to know that their wishes will be carried out and that all is in order gives each of you more freedom to meet this passage.

I help my parents and myself prepare for a good death.

Afterlife

When my grandparents died, we helped to clean out their house. From the combination of their papers and possessions, stories I knew, and others my mother remembered we built a portrait of their lives. Piecing together their fuller identities through dismantling their home, we all learned more about these wonderful people—Mike and Miriam Ross.

On the way home, I commented that it was ironic that I had a larger picture of them now that they were dead. As much as I loved and cherished my grandparents, it was only through their deaths that whole aspects of their existence were revealed to me. These new elements continue to inspire me today. And although I miss them deeply, I also carry them with me in ways that were beyond my limits when they were living.

Each of us is more than the sum of a single person's perspective or the limits of our life.

After All Is Said and Done

After taking care of my father almost daily for four years, I missed parentcare more than I expected once he died. It wasn't just that I didn't know how to start my morning without helping him get ready for day care. After a few weeks, I missed interacting with the health care professionals, the old folks that were his friends, and their families. We had a community.

I had changed in those years. Many of my defenses had come down. I knew my inner emotional life more deeply. I'd become less exacting toward myself and others. I was stronger and gentler at the same time. In general, I was more comfortable with myself. I was also exhausted—for many months afterward. It was as if I'd earned a Ph.D. in love.

Just as my father and mother helped me learn to walk as a baby, as an adult our time together helped me to push through many of my limited perceptions. They couldn't have left me a better gift. We came a long way from the relationship between adult and child, and now I understand the lifelong resources imbued within parents for their offspring.

I take the gifts I've received through practicing parentcare into the rest of my life.

Subject Index